To: _____

From: _____

God has given us his very great
and precious promises, so that through them
you may participate in the divine nature.
2 Peter 1:4

No matter how many promises God has made,
they are "yes" in Christ, and so through him
the "amen" is spoken by us to the glory of God.
2 Corinthians 1:20

November 23, 200?

Dear Mara,

Promises
for Mothers

from the new international version

formerly titled *Promises for Moms*

Love,
Mom

 ZONDERVAN®

 ZONDERVAN®

Promises for Mothers
Formerly titled *Promises for Moms* (ISBN: 0-310-98264-2)
Copyright © 2007 by Zondervan

Requests for information should be addressed to:

Zondervan, *Grand Rapids, Michigan* 49530

ISBN-10: 0-310-27868-6
ISBN-13: 978-0-310-27868-9

This edition printed on acid-free paper.

All Scripture quotations, unless otherwise indicated, are taken from
the *Holy Bible: New International Version*®. NIV®. Copyright © 1973,
1978, 1984 by International Bible Society. Used by permission of
Zondervan. All rights reserved.

All rights reserved. No part of this publication may be reproduced,
stored in a retrieval system, or transmitted in any form or by any
means — electronic, mechanical, photocopy, recording, or any
other — except for brief quotations in printed reviews, without the
prior permission of the publisher.

Interior design by Michelle Espinoza

Printed in China

07 08 09 10 11 12 • 15 14 13 12 11 10 9 8 7 6 5 4 3 2 1

Contents

Blessings	9
Children	17
Comfort	25
Courage	35
Decisions	41
Discernment	47
Encouragement	55
Faith	61
Forgiveness	65
Friendship	71
Future	75
God's Love	85
Grace	93
Guidance	101
Healing	107
Help	113
Home	121
Hope	131
Identity	137
Integrity	143
Joy	151

Marriage	161
Motherhood	167
Obedience	171
Patience	179
Peace	185
Perseverance	187
Praise and Worship	193
Prayer	197
Presence of God	205
Priorities	211
Protection	217
Provision	223
Rest	233
Salvation	241
Security	251
Strength	259
Trust	265
Unity	269
Wisdom	275
Worry	281
Work	287

Promises *for* Mothers

Blessings

Every good and perfect gift is from above, coming down from the Father of the heavenly lights, who does not change like shifting shadows.

James 1:17

From the fullness of God's grace we have all received one blessing after another.

John 1:16

Praise be to the God and Father of our Lord Jesus Christ, who has blessed us in the heavenly realms with every spiritual blessing in Christ.

Ephesians 1:3

You will eat the fruit of your labor;
blessings and prosperity will be yours.

Psalm 128:2

The LORD will open the heavens, the storehouse of his bounty, to send rain on your land in season and to bless all the work of your hands. You will lend to many nations but will borrow from none. The LORD will make you the head, not the tail. If you pay attention to the commands of the LORD your God that I give you this day and carefully follow them, you will always be at the top, never at the bottom.

Deuteronomy 28:12–13

The LORD had said to Abram, "Leave your country, your people and your father's household and go to the land I will show you.

"I will make you into a great nation
    and I will bless you;
I will make your name great,
    and you will be a blessing....
All peoples on earth
    will be blessed through you."

Genesis 12:1–3

God redeemed us in order that the blessing given to Abraham might come to the Gentiles through Christ Jesus, so that by faith we might receive the promise of the Spirit.

Galatians 3:14

The blessing of the LORD brings wealth,
    and he adds no trouble to it.

Proverbs 10:22

"I will pour water on the thirsty land, and streams on the dry ground; I will pour out my Spirit on your offspring, and my blessing on your descendants," says the Lord.

Isaiah 44:3

"I will bless [my people] and the places surrounding my hill. I will send down showers in season; there will be showers of blessing," says the Lord.

Ezekiel 34:26

"Bring the whole tithe into the storehouse, that there may be food in my house. Test me in this," says the LORD Almighty, "and see if I will not throw open the floodgates of heaven and pour out so much blessing that you will not have room enough for it."

Malachi 3:10

Worship the LORD your God, and his blessing will be on your food and water. I will take away sickness from among you.... I will give you a full life span.

Exodus 23:25–26

Do not repay evil with evil or insult with insult, but with blessing, because to this you were called so that you may inherit a blessing.

1 Peter 3:9

If you pay attention to these laws and are careful to follow them, then the LORD your God will keep his covenant of love with you, as he swore to your forefathers. He will love you and bless you and increase your numbers. He will bless the fruit of your womb, the crops of your land — your grain, new wine and oil — the calves of your herds and the lambs of your flocks in the land that he swore to your forefathers to give you. You will be blessed more than any other people; none of your men or women will be childless, nor any of your livestock without young.

Deuteronomy 7:12 – 14

In the presence of the LORD your God, you and your families shall eat and shall rejoice in everything you have put your hand to, because the LORD your God has blessed you.

Deuteronomy 12:7

My people will live in peaceful dwelling places,
    in secure homes,
    in undisturbed places of rest....
How blessed you will be.

Isaiah 32:18, 20

Be pleased to bless the house of your servant, that
it may continue forever in your sight; for you,
O Sovereign LORD, have spoken, and with your
blessing the house of your servant will be blessed
forever.

2 Samuel 7:29

A generous man will himself be blessed,
    for he shares his food with the poor.

Proverbs 22:9

The man who looks intently into the perfect law
that gives freedom, and continues to do this, not
forgetting what he has heard, but doing it — he
will be blessed in what he does.

James 1:25

Blessings crown the head of the righteous.

Proverbs 10:6

May you be blessed by the LORD,
 the Maker of heaven and earth.

Psalm 115:15

The Lord bless you
 and keep you; ...
The Lord turn his face toward you
 and give you peace.

Numbers 6:24, 26

Children

Sons are a heritage from the LORD,
　　children a reward from him.
Like arrows in the hands of a warrior
　　are sons born in one's youth.
Blessed is the man
　　whose quiver is full of them.

Psalm 127:3–5

Repent and be baptized, every one of you, in the
name of Jesus Christ for the forgiveness of your
sins. And you will receive the gift of the Holy
Spirit. The promise is for you and your children
and for all who are far off—for all whom the Lord
our God will call.

Acts 2:38–39

All your sons will be taught by the LORD,
　　and great will be your children's peace.

Isaiah 54:13

The Lord lifted the needy out of their affliction
and increased their families like flocks.

Psalm 107:41

Jesus said to them, "Let the little children come to
me, and do not hinder them, for the kingdom of
God belongs to such as these." . . . And he took the
children in his arms, put his hands on them and
blessed them.

Mark 10:14, 16

Train a child in the way he should go,
and when he is old he will not turn from it.

Proverbs 22:6

Children's children are a crown to the aged,
    and parents are the pride of their children.

Proverbs 17:6

From the lips of children and infants
    you have ordained praise, O Lord.

Psalm 8:2

From everlasting to everlasting
    the LORD's love is with those who fear him,
    and his righteousness with their children's
       children.

Psalm 103:17

"Fix these words of mine in your hearts and minds; tie them as symbols on your hands and bind them on your foreheads. Teach them to your children, talking about them when you sit at home and when you walk along the road, when you lie down and when you get up. Write them on the doorframes of your houses and on your gates, so that your days and the days of your children may be many in the land that the LORD swore to give your forefathers, as many as the days that the heavens are above the earth," says the Lord.

Deuteronomy 11:18–21

We will not hide them from their children;
    we will tell the next generation
the praiseworthy deeds of the LORD,
    his power, and the wonders he has done.
He decreed statutes for Jacob
    and established the law in Israel,
which he commanded our forefathers
    to teach their children,
so the next generation would know them,
    even the children yet to be born,
    and they in turn would tell their children.
Then they would put their trust in God
    and would not forget his deeds
    but would keep his commands.

Psalm 78:4–7

Blessed is the man who fears the LORD,
who finds great delight in his commands.
His children will be mighty in the land;
the generation of the upright will be blessed.

Psalm 112:1–2

The Lord settles the barren woman in her home
as a happy mother of children.

Psalm 113:9

May the LORD make you increase,
both you and your children.

Psalm 115:14

He who fears the LORD has a secure fortress,
and for his children it will be a refuge.

Proverbs 14:26

A wife of noble character who can find?
    She is worth far more than rubies.
Her children arise and call her blessed;
    her husband also, and he praises her.

Proverbs 31:10, 28

"I will give them singleness of heart and action, so that they will always fear me for their own good and the good of their children after them," says the Lord.

Jeremiah 32:39

I was young and now I am old,
    yet I have never seen the righteous forsaken
    or their children begging bread.
They are always generous and lend freely;
    their children will be blessed.

Psalm 37:25–26

Jesus took a little child and had him stand among them. Taking him in his arms, he said to them, "Whoever welcomes one of these little children in my name welcomes me; and whoever welcomes me does not welcome me but the one who sent me."

Mark 9:36–37

I have no greater joy than to hear that my children are walking in the truth.

3 John 4

Believe in the Lord Jesus, and you will be saved — you and your household.

Acts 16:31

Comfort

"As a mother comforts her child, so will I comfort you," says the Lord.

Isaiah 66:13

Cast your cares on the LORD
    and he will sustain you;
    he will never let the righteous fall.

Psalm 55:22

Jesus said, "In this world you will have trouble. But take heart! I have overcome the world."

John 16:33

The Lord heals the brokenhearted
    and binds up their wounds.

Psalm 147:3

Men are not cast off
　　by the Lord forever.
Though he brings grief, he will show compassion,
　　so great is his unfailing love.
For he does not willingly bring affliction
　　or grief to the children of men.

Lamentations 3:31–33

Praise be to the God and Father of our Lord Jesus
Christ, the Father of compassion and the God of
all comfort, who comforts us in all our troubles,
so that we can comfort those in any trouble with
the comfort we ourselves have received from God.
For just as the sufferings of Christ flow over into
our lives, so also through Christ our comfort
overflows.

2 Corinthians 1:3–5

The LORD himself goes before you and will be
with you; he will never leave you nor forsake you.
Do not be afraid; do not be discouraged.

Deuteronomy 31:8

Jesus said, "Blessed are those who mourn, for they
will be comforted."

Matthew 5:4

I will fear no evil,
    for you are with me,
your rod and your staff,
    they comfort me.

Psalm 23:4

The Lord has sent me to bind up the
        brokenhearted,
    to proclaim freedom for the captives
    and release from darkness for the prisoners,
to proclaim the year of the LORD's favor
    and the day of vengeance of our God,
to comfort all who mourn,
    and provide for those who grieve in Zion —
to bestow on them a crown of beauty
    instead of ashes,
the oil of gladness
    instead of mourning,
and a garment of praise
    instead of a spirit of despair.

Isaiah 61:1–3

Shout for joy, O heavens;
    rejoice, O earth;
    burst into song, O mountains!
For the LORD comforts his people
    and will have compassion on his afflicted ones.
Isaiah 49:13

The ransomed of the LORD will return.
They will enter Zion with singing;
    everlasting joy will crown their heads.
Gladness and joy will overtake them,
    and sorrow and sighing will flee away.
Isaiah 35:10

Those who sow in tears
    will reap with songs of joy.
He who goes out weeping,
    carrying seed to sow,
will return with songs of joy,
    carrying sheaves with him.

Psalm 126:5–6

    You will restore my life again;
from the depths of the earth
    you will again bring me up.
You will increase my honor
    and comfort me once again.

Psalm 71:20–21

I pray that out of God's glorious riches he may strengthen you with power through his Spirit in your inner being.

Ephesians 3:16

Jesus said, "Peace I leave with you; my peace I give you. I do not give to you as the world gives. Do not let your hearts be troubled and do not be afraid."

John 14:27

Jesus said, "Surely I am with you always, to the very end of the age."

Matthew 28:20

May your unfailing love be my comfort,
    according to your promise.

Psalm 119:76

The LORD is my light and my salvation—
    whom shall I fear?
The LORD is the stronghold of my life—
    of whom shall I be afraid?...
For in the day of trouble
    he will keep me safe in his dwelling;
he will hide me in the shelter of his tabernacle
    and set me high upon a rock....
I am still confident of this:
    I will see the goodness of the LORD
    in the land of the living.
Wait for the LORD;
    be strong and take heart
    and wait for the LORD.

Psalm 27:1, 5, 13–14

A righteous man may have many troubles,
  but the LORD delivers him from them all.

Psalm 34:19

The moon will shine like the sun, and the sunlight
will be seven times brighter, like the light of seven
full days, when the LORD binds up the bruises of
his people.

Isaiah 30:26

Cast all your anxiety on God because he cares for
you.

1 Peter 5:7

Courage

I can do everything through Christ who gives me strength.

Philippians 4:13

I eagerly expect and hope that I will in no way be ashamed, but will have sufficient courage so that now as always Christ will be exalted in my body.

Philippians 1:20

Christ is faithful as a son over God's house. And we are his house, if we hold on to our courage and the hope of which we boast.

Hebrews 3:6

When I called, you answered me;
    you made me bold and stouthearted.

Psalm 138:3

"Do not fear, for I am with you;
   do not be dismayed, for I am your God.
I will strengthen you and help you;
   I will uphold you with my righteous right
hand," says the Lord.

Isaiah 41:10

The wicked man flees though no one pursues,
   but the righteous are as bold as a lion.

Proverbs 28:1

"Be strong and courageous. Do not be terrified; do
not be discouraged, for the LORD your God will
be with you wherever you go," says the Lord.

Joshua 1:9

The righteous cry out, and the LORD hears them;
   he delivers them from all their troubles.

Psalm 34:17

This is what the LORD says—

"Fear not, for I have redeemed you;
I have summoned you by name;
    you are mine.

Isaiah 43:1

In Christ and through faith in him we may
approach God with freedom and confidence.

Ephesians 3:12

Jesus said, "Do not let your hearts be troubled.
Trust in God; trust also in me."

John 14:1

During the fourth watch of the night Jesus went
out to [his disciples], walking on the lake. When
the disciples saw him ... they were terrified. "It's a
ghost," they said, and cried out in fear. But Jesus
immediately said to them: "Take courage! It is I.
Don't be afraid."

Matthew 14:25–27

The eyes of the LORD are on the righteous
and his ears are attentive to their cry.

Psalm 34:15

Do not throw away your confidence; it will be
richly rewarded. You need to persevere so that
when you have done the will of God, you will
receive what he has promised.

Hebrews 10:35–36

The LORD is my light and my salvation —
whom shall I fear?
The LORD is the stronghold of my life —
of whom shall I be afraid?

Psalm 27:1

My purpose is that they may be encouraged in
heart and united in love, so that they may have
the full riches of complete understanding, in order
that they may know the mystery of God, namely,
Christ.

Colossians 2:2

In your unfailing love you will lead
    the people you have redeemed.
In your strength you will guide them
    to your holy dwelling.

Exodus 15:13

Decisions

Your word is a lamp to my feet, O Lord,
and a light for my path.

Psalm 119:105

If any of you lacks wisdom, he should ask God,
who gives generously to all without finding fault,
and it will be given to him.

James 1:5

The Lord guides me in paths of righteousness
for his name's sake.

Psalm 23:3

"I will counsel you and watch over you," says the
Lord.

Psalm 32:8

Jesus said, "When he, the Spirit of truth, comes, he will guide you into all truth. He will not speak on his own; he will speak only what he hears, and he will tell you what is yet to come."

John 16:13

You guide me with your counsel, O Lord,
    and afterward you will take me into glory.

Psalm 73:24

Trust in the LORD with all your heart
    and lean not on your own understanding;
in all your ways acknowledge him,
    and he will make your paths straight.

Proverbs 3:5–6

The lot is cast into the lap,
>   but its every decision is from the LORD.

Proverbs 16:33

Plans fail for lack of counsel,
>   but with many advisers they succeed.

Proverbs 15:22

God is our God for ever and ever;
>   he will be our guide even to the end.

Psalm 48:14

Let the morning bring me word of your unfailing
>   love,
>   for I have put my trust in you.
Show me the way I should go,
>   for to you I lift up my soul.

Psalm 143:8

Do not be anxious about anything, but in everything, by prayer and petition, with thanksgiving,
present your requests to God. And the peace of
God, which transcends all understanding, will
guard your hearts and your minds in Christ Jesus.

Philippians 4:6–7

Choose life, so that you and your children may
live and that you may love the LORD your God,
listen to his voice, and hold fast to him.

Deuteronomy 30:19–20

Let the wise listen and add to their learning,
    and let the discerning get guidance.

Proverbs 1:5

Jesus said, "The Counselor, the Holy Spirit, whom the Father will send in my name, will teach you all things and will remind you of everything I have said to you."

John 14:26

Jesus said, "So I say to you: Ask and it will be given to you; seek and you will find; knock and the door will be opened to you. For everyone who asks receives; he who seeks finds; and to him who knocks, the door will be opened."

Luke 11:9–10

Discernment

If you accept my words
    and store up my commands within you,
turning your ear to wisdom
    and applying your heart to understanding,
and if you call out for insight
    and cry aloud for understanding,
and if you look for it as for silver
    and search for it as for hidden treasure,
then you will understand the fear of the LORD
    and find the knowledge of God.

Proverbs 2:1–5

I am your servant; give me discernment
    that I may understand your statutes, O Lord.

Psalm 119:125

Solomon prayed, "Now, O LORD my God, you have made your servant king in place of my father David. But I am only a little child and not know how to carry out my duties. Your servant is here among the people you have chosen, a great people, too numerous to count or number. So give your servant a discerning heart to govern your people and to distinguish between right and wrong."

The Lord was pleased that Solomon had asked for this. So God said to him, "Since you have asked for this and not for long life or wealth for yourself, nor have asked for the death of your enemies but for discernment in administering justice, I will do what you have asked. I will give you a wise and discerning heart, so that there will never have been anyone like you, nor will there ever be. Moreover, I will give you what you have not asked for — both riches and honor — so that in your lifetime you will have no equal among kings."

1 Kings 3:7 – 13

The mocker seeks wisdom and finds none,
    but knowledge comes easily to the discerning.

Proverbs 14:6

The heart of the discerning acquires knowledge;
    the ears of the wise seek it out.

Proverbs 18:15

Each one should test his own actions. Then he can
take pride in himself, without comparing himself
to somebody else.

Galatians 6:4

Teach me knowledge and good judgment,
    for I believe in your commands, Lord.

Psalm 119:66

The Lord changes times and seasons;
>   he sets up kings and deposes them.
He gives wisdom to the wise
>   and knowledge to the discerning.

Daniel 2:21

The ways of the LORD are right;
>   the righteous walk in them.

Hosea 14:9

Gold there is, and rubies in abundance,
>   but lips that speak knowledge are a rare jewel.

Proverbs 20:15

This is my prayer: that your love may abound
more and more in knowledge and depth of insight,
so that you may be able to discern what is best and
may be pure and blameless until the day of Christ,
filled with the fruit of righteousness that comes
through Jesus Christ — to the glory and praise of
God.

Philippians 1:9–11

I have more insight than all my teachers,
    for I meditate on your statutes, Lord.

Psalm 119:99

The wise in heart are called discerning.

Proverbs 16:21

Jesus said, "The knowledge of the secrets of the kingdom of heaven has been given to you.... Whoever has will be given more, and he will have an abundance."

Matthew 13:11 – 12

God, who said, "Let light shine out of darkness," made his light shine in our hearts to give us the light of the knowledge of the glory of God in the face of Christ.

2 Corinthians 4:6

Since the day we heard about you, we have not stopped praying for you and asking God to fill you with the knowledge of his will through all spiritual wisdom and understanding.

Colossians 1:9

Preserve sound judgment and discernment,
    do not let them out of your sight;
they will be life for you,
    an ornament to grace your neck.

Proverbs 3:21–22

Encouragement

The Lord tends his flock like a shepherd:
    He gathers the lambs in his arms
and carries them close to his heart;
    he gently leads those that have young.

Isaiah 40:11

May our Lord Jesus Christ himself and God our Father, who loved us and by his grace gave us eternal encouragement and good hope, encourage your hearts and strengthen you in every good deed and word.

2 Thessalonians 2:16–17

Let us not give up meeting together, as some are in the habit of doing, but let us encourage one another—and all the more as you see the Day approaching.

Hebrews 10:25

My purpose is that they may be encouraged in
heart and united in love, so that they may have
the full riches of complete understanding, in order
that they may know the mystery of God, namely,
Christ, in whom are hidden all the treasures of
wisdom and knowledge.

Colossians 2:2–3

You are a shield around me, O LORD;
    you bestow glory on me and lift up my head.

Psalm 3:3

It is God who arms me with strength
    and makes my way perfect.
He makes my feet like the feet of a deer;
    he enables me to stand on the heights.

Psalm 18:32–33

I lift up my eyes to the hills—
    where does my help come from?
My help comes from the LORD,
    the Maker of heaven and earth.
He will not let your foot slip—
    he who watches over you will not slumber;
indeed, he who watches over Israel
    will neither slumber nor sleep.
The LORD watches over you—
    the LORD is your shade at your right hand;
the sun will not harm you by day,
    nor the moon by night.
The LORD will keep you from all harm—
    he will watch over your life;
the LORD will watch over your coming and going
    both now and forevermore.

Psalm 121:1–8

The Lord will cover you with his feathers,
    and under his wings you will find refuge;
his faithfulness will be your shield and rampart.

Psalm 91:4

You hear, O LORD, the desire of the afflicted;
    you encourage them, and you listen to their cry.

Psalm 10:17

In the day of trouble
    the Lord will keep me safe in his dwelling;
he will hide me in the shelter of his tabernacle
    and set me high upon a rock.

Psalm 27:5

If you make the Most High your dwelling—
   even the LORD, who is my refuge—
then no harm will befall you,
   no disaster will come near your tent.
For he will command his angels concerning you
   to guard you in all your ways;
they will lift you up in their hands,
   so that you will not strike your foot against a
      stone.

Psalm 91:9–12

Surely God is my help;
   the Lord is the one who sustains me.

Psalm 54:4

The LORD your God is with you,
    he is mighty to save.
He will take great delight in you,
    he will quiet you with his love,
he will rejoice over you with singing.

Zephaniah 3:17

The God of all grace, who called you to his eternal glory in Christ, after you have suffered a little while, will himself restore you and make you strong, firm and steadfast.

1 Peter 5:10

Faith

Everyone born of God overcomes the world. This is the victory that has overcome the world, even our faith.

1 John 5:4

The prayer offered in faith will make the sick person well; the Lord will raise him up. If he has sinned, he will be forgiven.

James 5:15

Have faith in the LORD your God and you will be upheld.

2 Chronicles 20:20

The LORD loves the just
    and will not forsake his faithful ones.
They will be protected forever.

Psalm 37:28

The LORD is good and his love endures forever;
   his faithfulness continues through all
      generations.

Psalm 100:5

The LORD rewards every man for his righteousness
and faithfulness.

1 Samuel 26:23

Though you have not seen Christ, you love him;
and even though you do not see him now, you
believe in him and are filled with an inexpressible
and glorious joy, for you are receiving the goal of
your faith, the salvation of your souls.

1 Peter 1:8–9

Praise be to the God and Father of our Lord Jesus Christ! In his great mercy he has given us new birth into a living hope through the resurrection of Jesus Christ from the dead, and into an inheritance that can never perish, spoil or fade—kept in heaven for you, who through faith are shielded by God's power until the coming of the salvation that is ready to be revealed in the last time.

1 Peter 1:3–5

Know therefore that the Lord your God is God; he is the faithful God, keeping his covenant of love to a thousand generations of those who love him and keep his commands.

Deuteronomy 7:9

Those who have served well gain an excellent standing and great assurance in their faith in Christ Jesus.

1 Timothy 3:13

All these people [Abraham, Noah, Isaac and
Jacob] were still living by faith when they died.
They did not receive the things promised; they
only saw them and welcomed them from a dis-
tance. And they admitted that they were aliens
and strangers on earth. People who say such things
show that they are looking for a country of their
own. If they had been thinking of the country
they had left, they would have had opportunity
to return. Instead, they were longing for a better
country — a heavenly one. Therefore God is not
ashamed to be called their God, for he has prepared a city for them.

Hebrews 11:13–16

I have fought the good fight, I have finished the
race, I have kept the faith. Now there is in store for
me the crown of righteousness, which the Lord,
the righteous Judge, will award to me on that
day — and not only to me, but also to all who have
longed for his appearing.

2 Timothy 4:7–8

Forgiveness

"If my people, who are called by my name, will humble themselves and pray and seek my face and turn from their wicked ways, then will I hear from heaven and will forgive their sin and will heal their land," says the Lord.

2 Chronicles 7:14

Jesus said, "When you stand praying, if you hold anything against anyone, forgive him, so that your Father in heaven may forgive you your sins."

Mark 11:25

"I will cleanse them from all the sin they have committed against me and will forgive all their sins of rebellion against me," says the Lord.

Jeremiah 33:8

If we confess our sins, God is faithful and just
and will forgive us our sins and purify us from all
unrighteousness.

1 John 1:9

Blessed is he
 whose transgressions are forgiven,
 whose sins are covered.
Blessed is the man
 whose sin the LORD does not count against him
 and in whose spirit is no deceit.

Psalm 32:1–2

If you, O LORD, kept a record of sins,
 O Lord, who could stand?
But with you there is forgiveness;
 therefore you are feared.

Psalm 130:3–4

Jesus told them, "This is what is written: The Christ will suffer and rise from the dead on the third day, and repentance and forgiveness of sins will be preached in his name to all nations, beginning at Jerusalem."

Luke 24:46–47

Repent and be baptized, every one of you, in the name of Jesus Christ for the forgiveness of your sins. And you will receive the gift of the Holy Spirit. The promise is for you and your children and for all who are far off—for all whom the Lord our God will call.

Acts 2:38–39

All the prophets testify about Christ that everyone who believes in him receives forgiveness of sins through his name.

Acts 10:43

In Christ we have redemption through his blood,
the forgiveness of sins, in accordance with the
riches of God's grace that he lavished on us with
all wisdom and understanding.

Ephesians 1:7–8

Praise the LORD, O my soul,
    and forget not all his benefits—
who forgives all your sins
    and heals all your diseases.

Psalm 103:2–3

Who is a God like you,
    who pardons sin and forgives the transgression
    of the remnant of his inheritance?
You do not stay angry forever
    but delight to show mercy.

Micah 7:18

God has rescued us from the dominion of darkness and brought us into the kingdom of the Son he loves, in whom we have redemption, the forgiveness of sins.

Colossians 1:13–14

You are forgiving and good, O Lord,
     abounding in love to all who call to you.

Psalm 86:5

I acknowledged my sin to you
     and did not cover up my iniquity.
I said, "I will confess
     my transgressions to the LORD" —
and you forgave
     the guilt of my sin.

Psalm 32:5

If you forgive men when they sin against you, your heavenly Father will also forgive you.

Matthew 6:14

Your sins have been forgiven on account of Christ's name.

1 John 2:12

Let us draw near to God with a sincere heart in full assurance of faith, having our hearts sprinkled to cleanse us from a guilty conscience and having our bodies washed with pure water. Let us hold unswervingly to the hope we profess, for he who promised is faithful.

Hebrews 10:22–23

Friendship

Jesus said, "I no longer call you servants, because a servant does not know his master's business. Instead, I have called you friends, for everything that I learned from my Father I have made known to you."

John 15:15

Jesus said, "Love each other as I have loved you. Greater love has no one than this, that he lay down his life for his friends."

John 15:12–13

There is a friend who sticks closer than a brother.

Proverbs 18:24

A friend loves at all times.

Proverbs 17:17

Go in peace, for we have sworn friendship with
each other in the name of the LORD, saying,
"The LORD is witness between you and me, and
between your descendants and my descendants
forever."

1 Samuel 20:42

My intercessor is my friend as my eyes pour out
tears to God; on behalf of a man he pleads with
God as a man pleads for his friend.

Job 16:20–21

Perfume and incense bring joy to the heart,
    and the pleasantness of one's friend springs
        from his earnest counsel.

Proverbs 27:9

Two are better than one, because they have a good
return for their work: If one falls down, his friend
can help him up.... Though one may be overpow-
ered, two can defend themselves. A cord of three
strands is not quickly broken.

Ecclesiastes 4:9–10, 12

A despairing man should have the devotion of his
friends.

Job 6:14

He who loves a pure heart and whose speech is
       gracious
  will have the king for his friend.

Proverbs 22:11

Wounds from a friend can be trusted.

Proverbs 27:6

"I led them with cords of human kindness, with ties of love; I lifted the yoke from their neck and bent down to feed them," says the Lord.

Hosea 11:4

He who walks with the wise grows wise.

Proverbs 13:20

Future

Trust in the LORD with all your heart
> and lean not on your own understanding;
in all your ways acknowledge him,
> and he will make your paths straight.

Proverbs 3:5–6

"I know the plans I have for you," declares the
LORD, "plans to prosper you and not to harm you,
plans to give you hope and a future."

Jeremiah 29:11

If the LORD delights in a man's way,
> he makes his steps firm.

Psalm 37:23

Commit your way to the LORD;
    trust in him and he will do this:
He will make your righteousness shine like the
        dawn,
    the justice of your cause like the noonday sun.

Psalm 37:5 – 6

Jesus said, "In the future you will see the Son of
Man sitting at the right hand of the Mighty One
and coming on the clouds of heaven."

Matthew 26:64

In his heart a man plans his course,
    but the LORD determines his steps.

Proverbs 16:9

Delight yourself in the LORD
    and he will give you the desires of your heart.

Psalm 37:4

Do not let this Book of the Law depart from your
mouth; meditate on it day and night, so that you
may be careful to do everything written in it.
Then you will be prosperous and successful.

Joshua 1:8

Be confident of this, that God who began a good
work in you will carry it on to completion until
the day of Christ Jesus.

Philippians 1:6

Consider the blameless, observe the upright;
 there is a future for the man of peace.

Psalm 37:37

Wisdom is sweet to your soul;
 if you find it, there is a future hope for you,
 and your hope will not be cut off.

Proverbs 24:14

Jesus said, "When he, the Spirit of truth, comes,
he will ... not speak on his own; he will speak
only what he hears, and he will tell you what is yet
to come."

John 16:13

Commit to the LORD whatever you do,
and your plans will succeed.

Proverbs 16:3

Be strong and courageous. Do not be terrified; do
not be discouraged, for the LORD your God will
be with you wherever you go.

Joshua 1:9

The righteousness of the blameless makes a
straight way for them.

Proverbs 11:5

You need to persevere so that when you have done
the will of God, you will receive what he has
promised.

Hebrews 10:36

Posterity will serve him;
> future generations will be told about the Lord.

Psalm 22:30

The world and its desires pass away, but the man who does the will of God lives forever.

1 John 2:17

The Lord is not slow in keeping his promise, as some understand slowness. He is patient with you, not wanting anyone to perish, but everyone to come to repentance.

2 Peter 3:9

"I make known the end from the beginning,
    from ancient times, what is still to come.
I say: My purpose will stand,
    and I will do all that I please," says the Lord.

Isaiah 46:10

It is God who makes ... you stand firm in Christ.
He anointed us, set his seal of ownership on us,
and put his Spirit in our hearts as a deposit, guaranteeing what is to come.

2 Corinthians 1:21 – 22

[A wife of noble character] is clothed with strength
        and dignity;
    she can laugh at the days to come.

Proverbs 31:25

Jesus said, "Since you have kept my command to endure patiently, I will also keep you from the hour of trial that is going to come upon the whole world to test those who live on the earth."

Revelation 3:10

No eye has seen,
    no ear has heard,
no mind has conceived
    what God has prepared for those who love him.
1 Corinthians 2:9

The LORD will fulfill his purpose for me;
    your love, O LORD, endures forever.
Psalm 138:8

One of the seven angels ... came and said to me, "Come, I will show you the bride, the wife of the Lamb."

And he carried me away in the Spirit to a mountain great and high, and showed me the Holy City, Jerusalem, coming down out of heaven from God. It shone with the glory of God, and its brilliance was like that of a very precious jewel, like a jasper, clear as crystal.

Revelation 21:9–11

"Forget the former things;
 do not dwell on the past.
See, I am doing a new thing!
 Now it springs up; do you not perceive it?
I am making a way in the desert
 and streams in the wasteland," says the Lord.

Isaiah 43:18–19

I saw a new heaven and a new earth, for the first heaven and the first earth had passed away, and there was no longer any sea. I saw the Holy City, the new Jerusalem, coming down out of heaven from God, prepared as a bride beautifully dressed for her husband. And I heard a loud voice from the throne saying, "Now the dwelling of God is with men, and he will live with them. They will be his people, and God himself will be with them and be their God. He will wipe every tear from their eyes. There will be no more death or mourning or crying or pain, for the old order of things has passed away."

He who was seated on the throne said, "I am making everything new!"

Revelation 21:1–5

God's Love

This is how we know what love is: Jesus Christ laid down his life for us.

1 John 3:16

Surely goodness and love will follow me
    all the days of my life,
and I will dwell in the house of the LORD forever.

Psalm 23:6

How great is the love the Father has lavished on us, that we should be called children of God!

1 John 3:1

May your unfailing love rest upon us, O LORD,
    even as we put our hope in you.

Psalm 33:22

It was just before the Passover Feast. Jesus knew that the time had come for him to leave this world and go to the Father. Having loved his own who were in the world, he now showed them the full extent of his love.

John 13:1

Your love, O LORD, reaches to the heavens,
   your faithfulness to the skies.

Psalm 36:5

Love is patient, love is kind. It does not envy, it does not boast, it is not proud. It is not rude, it is not self-seeking, it is not easily angered, it keeps no record of wrongs. Love does not delight in evil but rejoices with the truth. It always protects, always trusts, always hopes, always perseveres. Love never fails.

1 Corinthians 13:4–8

I pray that you, being rooted and established in love, may have power, together with all the saints, to grasp how wide and long and high and deep is the love of Christ, and to know this love that surpasses knowledge—that you may be filled to the measure of all the fullness of God.

Ephesians 3:17–19

I trust in your unfailing love;
     my heart rejoices in your salvation.

Psalm 13:5

You are a forgiving God, gracious and compassion-ate, slow to anger and abounding in love.

Nehemiah 9:17

"Though the mountains be shaken
    and the hills be removed,
yet my unfailing love for you will not be shaken
    nor my covenant of peace be removed,"
    says the LORD, who has compassion on you.

Isaiah 54:10

Because of the LORD's great love we are not consumed, for his compassions never fail.

Lamentations 3:22

Know ... that the LORD your God is God; he is
the faithful God, keeping his covenant of love to
a thousand generations of those who love him and
keep his commands.

Deuteronomy 7:9

This is how God showed his love among us: He
sent his one and only Son into the world that we
might live through him. This is love: not that we
loved God, but that he loved us and sent his Son
as an atoning sacrifice for our sins.

1 John 4:9–10

God is love. Whoever lives in love lives in God,
and God in him.

1 John 4:16

As high as the heavens are above the earth,
    so great is God's love for those who fear him.

Psalm 103:11

God has poured out his love into our hearts by the Holy Spirit, whom he has given us.

Romans 5:5

God demonstrates his own love for us in this: While we were still sinners, Christ died for us.

Romans 5:8

I am convinced that neither death nor life, neither angels nor demons, neither the present nor the future, nor any powers, neither height nor depth, nor anything else in all creation, will be able to separate us from the love of God that is in Christ Jesus our Lord.

Romans 8:38–39

When the kindness and love of God our Savior
appeared, he saved us, not because of righteous
things we had done, but because of his mercy.

Titus 3:4–5

From everlasting to everlasting
    the LORD's love is with those who fear him,
and his righteousness with their
    children's children.

Psalm 103:17

Greater love has no one than this, that he lay
down his life for his friends.

John 15:13

Grace, mercy and peace from God the Father and from Jesus Christ, the Father's Son, will be with us in truth and love.

2 John 1:3

God did not give us a spirit of timidity, but a spirit of power, of love and of self-discipline.

2 Timothy 1:7

Because of his great love for us, God, who is rich in mercy, made us alive with Christ even when we were dead in transgressions—it is by grace you have been saved.

Ephesians 2:4–5

Grace

Praise be to the God and Father of our Lord Jesus
Christ, who has blessed us in the heavenly realms
with every spiritual blessing in Christ. For he
chose us in him before the creation of the world
to be holy and blameless in his sight. In love he
predestined us to be adopted as his sons through
Jesus Christ, in accordance with his pleasure and
will — to the praise of his glorious grace, which he
has freely given us in the One he loves. In him we
have redemption through his blood, the forgiveness of sins, in accordance with the riches of God's
grace that he lavished on us with all wisdom and
understanding.

Ephesians 1:3–8

From the fullness of God's grace we have all
received one blessing after another.

John 1:16

I commit you to God and to the word of his grace, which can build you up and give you an inheritance among all those who are sanctified.

Acts 20:32

Now a righteousness from God, apart from law, has been made known, to which the Law and the Prophets testify. This righteousness from God comes through faith in Jesus Christ to all who believe. There is no difference, for all have sinned and fall short of the glory of God, and are justified freely by his grace through the redemption that came by Christ Jesus.

Romans 3:21–24

By the grace of God I am what I am, and his grace to me was not without effect.

1 Corinthians 15:10

God raised us up with Christ and seated us with him in the heavenly realms in Christ Jesus, in order that in the coming ages he might show the incomparable riches of his grace, expressed in his kindness to us in Christ Jesus. For it is by grace you have been saved, through faith — and this not from yourselves, it is the gift of God.

Ephesians 2:6–8

God mocks proud mockers but gives grace to the humble.

Proverbs 3:34

The Lord your God is gracious and compassionate. He will not turn his face from you if you return to him.

2 Chronicles 30:9

When the kindness and love of God our Savior appeared, he saved us, not because of righteous things we had done, but because of his mercy. He saved us through the washing of rebirth and renewal by the Holy Spirit, whom he poured out on us generously through Jesus Christ our Savior, so that, having been justified by his grace, we might become heirs having the hope of eternal life.

Titus 3:4–7

The Word became flesh and made his dwelling among us. We have seen his glory, the glory of the One and Only, who came from the Father, full of grace and truth.

John 1:14

If the many died by the trespass of the one man, how much more did God's grace and the gift that came by the grace of the one man, Jesus Christ, overflow to the many!

Romans 5:15

You know the grace of our Lord Jesus Christ, that though he was rich, yet for your sakes he became poor, so that you through his poverty might become rich.

2 Corinthians 8:9

The gracious hand of our God is on everyone who looks to him.

Ezra 8:22

God is able to make all grace abound to you, so
that in all things at all times, having all that you
need, you will abound in every good work.

2 Corinthians 9:8

Jesus said, "My grace is sufficient for you, for my
power is made perfect in weakness."

2 Corinthians 12:9

May God be gracious to us and bless us
    and make his face shine upon us.

Psalm 67:1

To each one of us grace has been given as Christ apportioned it.

Ephesians 4:7

The grace of our Lord was poured out on me abundantly, along with the faith and love that are in Christ Jesus.

1 Timothy 1:14

God's grace was given us in Christ Jesus before the beginning of time.

2 Timothy 1:9

The grace of God that brings salvation has appeared to all men.

Titus 2:11

Let us ... approach the throne of grace with confidence, so that we may receive mercy and find grace to help us in our time of need.

Hebrews 4:16

The LORD make his face shine upon you and be gracious to you.

Numbers 6:25

Guidance

"I will instruct you and teach you in the way you should go," says the Lord.

Psalm 32:8

Whether you turn to the right or to the left, your ears will hear a voice behind you, saying, "This is the way; walk in it."

Isaiah 30:21

You guide me with your counsel, Lord,
 and afterward you will take me into glory.

Psalm 73:24

Plans fail for lack of counsel,
 but with many advisers they succeed.

Proverbs 15:22

"I guide you in the way of wisdom
    and lead you along straight paths," says the
    Lord.

Proverbs 4:11

The LORD will guide you always;
    he will satisfy your needs in a sun-scorched
        land
    and will strengthen your frame.
You will be like a well-watered garden,
    like a spring whose waters never fail.

Isaiah 58:11

Your word is a lamp to my feet, O Lord,
    and a light for my path.

Psalm 119:105

Show me your ways, O LORD,
    teach me your paths;
guide me in your truth and teach me,
    for you are God my Savior,
    and my hope is in you all day long.
                                        Psalm 25:4–5

Since you are my rock and my fortress, Lord,
    for the sake of your name lead and guide me.
                                        Psalm 31:3

Send forth your light and your truth,
    let them guide me, O God;
let them bring me to your holy mountain,
    to the place where you dwell.

                                        Psalm 43:3

If I go up to the heavens, you are there, O Lord;
    if I make my bed in the depths, you are there.
If I rise on the wings of the dawn,
    if I settle on the far side of the sea,
even there your hand will guide me,
    your right hand will hold me fast.

Psalm 139:8–10

    The Lord makes me lie down in green pastures,
he leads me beside quiet waters,
    he restores my soul.
He guides me in paths of righteousness
    for his name's sake.

Psalm 23:2–3

Teach me to do your will,
    for you are my God;
may your good Spirit
    lead me on level ground.

Psalm 143:10

"I will give you shepherds after my own heart, who will lead you with knowledge and understanding," says the Lord.

Jeremiah 3:15

For lack of guidance a nation falls,
    but many advisers make victory sure.

Proverbs 11:14

The Lord stilled the storm to a whisper;
　　the waves of the sea were hushed.
They were glad when it grew calm,
　　and he guided them to their desired haven.

Psalm 107:29–30

May the Lord direct your hearts into God's love
and Christ's perseverance.

2 Thessalonians 3:5

Healing

The Messiah was pierced for our transgressions,
he was crushed for our iniquities; the punishment
that brought us peace was upon him, and by his
wounds we are healed.

Isaiah 53:5

"For you who revere my name, the sun of righteousness will rise with healing in its wings," says
the Lord.

Malachi 4:2

"I will heal my people and will let them enjoy
abundant peace and security," says the Lord.

Jeremiah 33:6

As Jesus was on his way, the crowds almost crushed him. And a woman was there who had been subject to bleeding for twelve years, but no one could heal her. She came up behind him and touched the edge of his cloak, and immediately her bleeding stopped.

"Who touched me?" Jesus asked.

When they all denied it, Peter said, "Master, the people are crowding and pressing against you."

But Jesus said, "Someone touched me; I know that power has gone out from me."

Then the woman, seeing that she could not go unnoticed, came trembling and fell at his feet. In the presence of all the people, she told why she had touched him and how she had been instantly healed. Then he said to her, "Daughter, your faith has healed you. Go in peace."

Luke 8:42–48

Reckless words pierce like a sword,
  but the tongue of the wise brings healing.

Proverbs 12:18

Pleasant words are a honeycomb,
  sweet to the soul and healing to the bones.

Proverbs 16:24

I am the LORD, who heals you.

Exodus 15:26

O LORD my God, I called to you for help
  and you healed me.

Psalm 30:2

Is not this the kind of fasting I have chosen: to loose the chains of injustice and untie the cords of the yoke, to set the oppressed free and break every yoke?... Then your light will break forth like the dawn, and your healing will quickly appear.

Isaiah 58:6, 8

Praise the LORD, O my soul,
     and forget not all his benefits—
who forgives all your sins
     and heals all your diseases.

Psalm 103:2–3

Wherever Jesus went — into villages, towns or countryside — they placed the sick in the market-places. They begged him to let them touch even the edge of his cloak, and all who touched him were healed.

Mark 6:56

The Lord heals the brokenhearted
and binds up their wounds.

Psalm 147:3

Confess your sins to each other and pray for each other so that you may be healed. The prayer of a righteous man is powerful and effective.

James 5:16

Jesus himself bore our sins in his body on the tree, so that we might die to sins and live for righteousness; by his wounds you have been healed.

1 Peter 2:24

Do not be wise in your own eyes;
    fear the LORD and shun evil.
This will bring health to your body
    and nourishment to your bones.

Proverbs 3:7–8

Pay attention to what I say;
    listen closely to my words.
Do not let them out of your sight,
    keep them within your heart;
for they are life to those who find them
    and health to a man's whole body.

Proverbs 4:20–22

Dear friend, I pray that you may enjoy good
health and that all may go well with you, even as
your soul is getting along well.

3 John 2

Help

God is our refuge and strength,
    an ever-present help in trouble.

Psalm 46:1

You are my lamp, O LORD;
    the LORD turns my darkness into light.
With your help I can advance against a troop;
    with my God I can scale a wall.

2 Samuel 22:29–30

The LORD said to Moses, "Now go; I will help you
speak and will teach you what to say."

Exodus 4:12

In my distress I called to the LORD;
    I cried to my God for help.
From his temple he heard my voice;
    my cry came before him, into his ears.

Psalm 18:6

Surely God is my help;
    the Lord is the one who sustains me.

Psalm 54:4

The Lord has not despised or disdained
    the suffering of the afflicted one;
he has not hidden his face from him
    but has listened to his cry for help.

Psalm 22:24

We wait in hope for the LORD;
    he is our help and our shield.

Psalm 33:20

Because Jesus himself suffered when he was
tempted, he is able to help those who are being
tempted.

Hebrews 2:18

Because you are my help,
>   I sing in the shadow of your wings, O Lord.
My soul clings to you;
>   your right hand upholds me.

Psalm 63:7–8

Let us ... approach the throne of grace with confidence, so that we may receive mercy and find grace to help us in our time of need.

Hebrews 4:16

How gracious God will be when you cry for help! As soon as he hears, he will answer you.

Isaiah 30:19

Do not fear, for I am with you; do not be dismayed, for I am your God. I will strengthen you and help you; I will uphold you with my righteous right hand.... For I am the LORD, your God, who takes hold of your right hand and says to you, Do not fear; I will help you.

Isaiah 41:10, 13

You will call, and the LORD will answer; you will cry for help, and he will say: Here am I.

Isaiah 58:9

I lift up my eyes to the hills—
    where does my help come from?
My help comes from the LORD,
    the Maker of heaven and earth.
He will not let your foot slip—
    he who watches over you will not slumber;
indeed, he who watches over Israel
    will neither slumber nor sleep.
The LORD watches over you—
    the LORD is your shade at your right hand;
the sun will not harm you by day,
    nor the moon by night.
The LORD will keep you from all harm—
    he will watch over your life;
the LORD will watch over your coming and going
    both now and forevermore.

Psalm 121:1–8

The Spirit helps us in our weakness. We do not
know what we ought to pray for, but the Spirit
himself intercedes for us with groans that words
cannot express.

Romans 8:26

You, O God, do see trouble and grief;
    you consider it to take it in hand.
The victim commits himself to you;
    you are the helper of the fatherless.

Psalm 10:14

The LORD is with me;
    he is my helper.

Psalm 118:7

The LORD is my strength and my shield;
    my heart trusts in him, and I am helped.
My heart leaps for joy
    and I will give thanks to him in song.

Psalm 28:7

For God says,
    "In the time of my favor I heard you, and in
the day of salvation I helped you."
    I tell you, now is the time of God's favor, now
is the day of salvation.

2 Corinthians 6:2

Home

As for me and my household, we will serve the
LORD.

Joshua 24:15

Even the sparrow has found a home,
    and the swallow a nest for herself,
    where she may have her young —
a place near your altar,
    O LORD Almighty, my King and my God.

Psalm 84:3

Long life to you! Good health to you and your
household! And good health to all that is yours!

1 Samuel 25:6

These commandments that I give you today are to be upon your hearts. Impress them on your children. Talk about them when you sit at home and when you walk along the road, when you lie down and when you get up. Tie them as symbols on your hands and bind them on your foreheads. Write them on the doorframes of your houses and on your gates....

Do what is right and good in the LORD's sight, so that it may go well with you and you may go in and take over the good land that the LORD promised on oath to your forefathers.

Deuteronomy 6:6–9, 18

"I will provide a place for my people Israel and will plant them so that they can have a home of their own and no longer be disturbed," says the Lord.

2 Samuel 7:10

The Lord settles the barren woman in her home
     as a happy mother of children.

Psalm 113:9

The LORD blesses the home of the righteous.

Proverbs 3:33

Jesus replied, "If anyone loves me, he will obey my
teaching. My Father will love him, and we will
come to him and make our home with him."

John 14:23

"I will gather you; ... I will bring you home. I will
give you honor and praise among all the peoples of
the earth when I restore your fortunes before your
very eyes," says the LORD.

Zephaniah 3:20

In keeping with God's promise we are looking forward to a new heaven and a new earth, the home of righteousness.

2 Peter 3:13

"I tell you the truth," Jesus [said], "no one who has left home or brothers or sisters or mother or father or children or fields for me and the gospel will fail to receive a hundred times as much in this present age (homes, brothers, sisters, mothers, children and fields—and with them, persecutions) and in the age to come, eternal life."

Mark 10:29–30

In the house of the wise are stores of choice food and oil.

Proverbs 21:20

As Jesus and his disciples were on their way, he came to a village where a woman named Martha opened her home to him. She had a sister called Mary, who sat at the Lord's feet listening to what he said. But Martha was distracted by all the preparations that had to be made. She came to him and asked, "Lord, don't you care that my sister has left me to do the work by myself? Tell her to help me!"

"Martha, Martha," the Lord answered, "you are worried and upset about many things, but only one thing is needed. Mary has chosen what is better, and it will not be taken away from her."

Luke 10:38–42

Your sons will be like olive shoots
    around your table.
Thus is the man blessed
    who fears the Lord.

Psalm 128:3–4

By wisdom a house is built,
    and through understanding it is established;
through knowledge its rooms are filled
    with rare and beautiful treasures.

Proverbs 24:3–4

In Christ you too are being built together to
become a dwelling in which God lives by his
Spirit.

Ephesians 2:22

Jesus said, "Everyone who hears these words of mine and puts them into practice is like a wise man who built his house on the rock. The rain came down, the streams rose, and the winds blew and beat against that house; yet it did not fall, because it had its foundation on the rock."

Matthew 7:24–25

Jesus said, "In my Father's house are many rooms; if it were not so, I would have told you. I am going there to prepare a place for you. And if I go and prepare a place for you, I will come back and take you to be with me that you also may be where I am."

John 14:2–3

As you come to Christ, the living Stone—rejected by men but chosen by God and precious to him—you also, like living stones, are being built into a spiritual house to be a holy priesthood, offering spiritual sacrifices acceptable to God through Jesus Christ.

1 Peter 2:4–5

Believe in the Lord Jesus, and you will be saved—you and your household.

Acts 16:31

Lord, you have been our dwelling place
    throughout all generations.

Psalm 90:1

If you make the Most High your dwelling—
    even the LORD, who is my refuge—
then no harm will befall you,
    no disaster will come near your tent.

Psalm 91:9–10

"My people will live in peaceful dwelling places, in secure homes, in undisturbed places of rest," says the Lord.

Isaiah 32:18

Hope

Find rest, O my soul, in God alone;
    my hope comes from him.

Psalm 62:5

No one whose hope is in you, Lord,
    will ever be put to shame.

Psalm 25:3

The eyes of the LORD are on those who fear him,
    on those whose hope is in his unfailing love.

Psalm 33:18

The LORD is good to those whose hope is in him,
to the one who seeks him.

Lamentations 3:25

Discipline your son,
    for in that there is hope....
Discipline your son,
    and he will give you peace;
he will bring delight to your soul.

Proverbs 19:18; 29:17

Do any of the worthless idols of the nations bring rain? Do the skies themselves send down showers?

No, it is you, O Lord our God. Therefore our hope is in you, for you are the one who does all this.

Jeremiah 14:22

Everything that was written in the past was written to teach us, so that through endurance and the encouragement of the Scriptures we might have hope.

Romans 15:4

This I call to mind and therefore I have hope: Because of the LORD's great love we are not consumed, for his compassions never fail.

Lamentations 3:21–22

Dear friends, now we are children of God, and what we will be has not yet been made known. But we know that when he appears, we shall be like him, for we shall see him as he is. Everyone who has this hope in him purifies himself, just as he is pure.

1 John 3:2–3

You have been my hope, O Sovereign LORD,
my confidence since my youth.

Psalm 71:5

We have heard of your faith in Christ Jesus ...
faith and love that spring from the hope that is
stored up for you in heaven and that you have
already heard about in the word of truth, the
gospel.

Colossians 1:4–5

Praise be to the God and Father of our Lord Jesus
Christ! In his great mercy he has given us new
birth into a living hope through the resurrection
of Jesus Christ from the dead.

1 Peter 1:3

May your unfailing love rest upon us, O LORD,
even as we put our hope in you.

Psalm 33:22

God has delivered us from such a deadly peril, and he will deliver us. On him we have set our hope that he will continue to deliver us.

2 Corinthians 1:10

We have put our hope in the living God, who is the Savior of all men, and especially of those who believe.

1 Timothy 4:10

May those who fear you, Lord, rejoice when they
    see me,
    for I have put my hope in your word....
You are my refuge and my shield;
    I have put my hope in your word.

Psalm 119:74, 114

Our sons in their youth
    will be like well-nurtured plants,
and our daughters will be like pillars
    carved to adorn a palace....
Blessed are the people of whom this is true;
    blessed are the people whose God is the LORD.

Psalm 144:12, 15

Train a child in the way he should go,
    and when he is old he will not turn from it.

Proverbs 22:6

Identity

I praise you, Lord, because I am fearfully and
 wonderfully made;
your works are wonderful,
I know that full well.

Psalm 139:14

We are God's workmanship, created in Christ
Jesus to do good works, which God prepared in
advance for us to do.

Ephesians 2:10

As a bridegroom rejoices over his bride, so will
your God rejoice over you.

Isaiah 62:5

The LORD your God is with you,
    he is mighty to save.
He will take great delight in you,
    he will quiet you with his love,
he will rejoice over you with singing.

Zephaniah 3:17

God made Christ who had no sin to be sin for us,
so that in him we might become the righteousness
of God.

2 Corinthians 5:21

I will give them a heart to know me, that I am the
LORD. They will be my people, and I will be their
God.

Jeremiah 24:7

My frame was not hidden from you, Lord,
    when I was made in the secret place.
When I was woven together in the depths of the
            earth,
    your eyes saw my unformed body.
All the days ordained for me
    were written in your book
    before one of them came to be.

Psalm 139:15–16

God made my mouth like a sharpened sword, in
the shadow of his hand he hid me; he made me
into a polished arrow and concealed me in his
quiver.

Isaiah 49:2

"Before I formed you in the womb I knew you,
before you were born I set you apart," says the
Lord.

Jeremiah 1:5

You brought me out of the womb, Lord;
　　you made me trust in you
　　even at my mother's breast.
From birth I was cast upon you;
　　from my mother's womb you have been my
　　　　God.

Psalm 22:9–10

In Christ we who are many form one body, and
each member belongs to all the others. We have
different gifts, according to the grace given us.

Romans 12:5–6

O Lord, you have searched me
    and you know me.
You know when I sit and when I rise;
    you perceive my thoughts from afar.
You discern my going out and my lying down;
    you are familiar with all my ways.

Psalm 139:1–3

If anyone is in Christ, he is a new creation; the old
has gone, the new has come!

2 Corinthians 5:17

You are all sons of God through faith in Christ
Jesus, for all of you who were baptized into Christ
have clothed yourselves with Christ. There is
neither Jew nor Greek, slave nor free, male nor
female, for you are all one in Christ Jesus. If you
belong to Christ, then you are Abraham's seed,
and heirs according to the promise.

Galatians 3:26–29

We are God's fellow workers; you are God's field, God's building.

1 Corinthians 3:9

The Spirit himself testifies with our spirit that we are God's children.

Romans 8:16

How great is the love the Father has lavished on us, that we should be called children of God! And that is what we are!

1 John 3:1

We, who with unveiled faces all reflect the Lord's glory, are being transformed into his likeness with ever-increasing glory, which comes from the Lord, who is the Spirit.

2 Corinthians 3:18

Integrity

For the LORD God is a sun and shield;
   the LORD bestows favor and honor;
no good thing does he withhold
   from those whose walk is blameless.

Psalm 84:11

Blessed are they whose ways are blameless,
   who walk according to the law of the LORD.
Blessed are they who keep his statutes
   and seek him with all their heart.

Psalm 119:1–2

In my integrity you uphold me, Lord,
   and set me in your presence forever.

Psalm 41:12

The man of integrity walks securely.

Proverbs 10:9

The integrity of the upright guides them.

Proverbs 11:3

My salvation and my honor depend on God;
   he is my mighty rock, my refuge.

Psalm 62:7

Those who walk uprightly enter into peace.

Isaiah 57:2

This is my prayer: that your love may abound
more and more in knowledge and depth of insight,
so that you may be able to discern what is best and
may be pure and blameless until the day of Christ,
filled with the fruit of righteousness that comes
through Jesus Christ — to the glory and praise of
God.

Philippians 1:9–11

LORD, who may dwell in your sanctuary?
    Who may live on your holy hill?
He whose walk is blameless
    and who does what is righteous,
who speaks the truth from his heart.

Psalm 15:1–2

Keep your servant ... from willful sins, Lord;
    may they not rule over me.
Then will I be blameless,
    innocent of great transgression.
May the words of my mouth and the meditation
       of my heart
    be pleasing in your sight,
    O LORD, my Rock and my Redeemer.

Psalm 19:13 – 14

The upright will live in the land,
    and the blameless will remain in it.

Proverbs 2:21

The Lord holds victory in store for the upright,
  he is a shield to those whose walk is blameless,
for he guards the course of the just
  and protects the way of his faithful ones.

Proverbs 2:7–8

God will keep you strong to the end, so that you
will be blameless on the day of our Lord Jesus
Christ.

1 Corinthians 1:8

May God strengthen your hearts so that you will
be blameless and holy in the presence of our God
and Father when our Lord Jesus comes with all his
holy ones.

1 Thessalonians 3:13

May God himself, the God of peace, sanctify you through and through. May your whole spirit, soul and body be kept blameless at the coming of our Lord Jesus Christ. The one who calls you is faithful and he will do it.

1 Thessalonians 5:23–24

The LORD is righteous,
 he loves justice;
 upright men will see his face.

Psalm 11:7

Consider the blameless, observe the upright;
  there is a future for the man of peace.

Psalm 37:37

Light is shed upon the righteous
  and joy on the upright in heart.

Psalm 97:11

Even in darkness light dawns for the upright,
  for the gracious and compassionate and righteous man.

Psalm 112:4

Joy

The LORD your God will bless you in all your harvest and in all the work of your hands, and your joy will be complete.

Deuteronomy 16:15

The joy of the LORD is your strength.

Nehemiah 8:10

The Lord will yet fill your mouth with laughter and your lips with shouts of joy.

Job 8:21

The precepts of the LORD are right,
	giving joy to the heart.
The commands of the LORD are radiant,
	giving light to the eyes.

Psalm 19:8

Let all who take refuge in you be glad, Lord;
    let them ever sing for joy.
Spread your protection over them,
    that those who love your name may rejoice
        in you.

Psalm 5:11

You have made known to me the path of life,
        O Lord;
    you will fill me with joy in your presence,
    with eternal pleasures at your right hand.

Psalm 16:11

A cheerful look brings joy to the heart.

Proverbs 15:30

Jesus said, "The kingdom of heaven is like treasure hidden in a field. When a man found it, he hid it again, and then in his joy went and sold all he had and bought that field."

Matthew 13:44

The bride belongs to the bridegroom. The friend who attends the bridegroom waits and listens for him, and is full of joy when he hears the bridegroom's voice. That joy is mine, and it is now complete.

John 3:29

Jesus said, "As the Father has loved me, so have I loved you. Now remain in my love. If you obey my commands, you will remain in my love, just as I have obeyed my Father's commands and remain in his love. I have told you this so that my joy may be in you and that your joy may be complete."

John 15:9–11

God has shown kindness by giving you rain from heaven and crops in their seasons; he provides you with plenty of food and fills your hearts with joy.

Acts 14:17

Though you have not seen Christ, you love him;
and even though you do not see him now, you
believe in him and are filled with an inexpressible
and glorious joy, for you are receiving the goal of
your faith, the salvation of your souls.

1 Peter 1:8–9

You will go out in joy
    and be led forth in peace;
the mountains and hills
    will burst into song before you,
and all the trees of the field
    will clap their hands.

Isaiah 55:12

In God our hearts rejoice,
    for we trust in his holy name.

Psalm 33:21

Those who sow in tears
    will reap with songs of joy.
He who goes out weeping,
    carrying seed to sow,
will return with songs of joy,
    carrying sheaves with him.

Psalm 126:5–6

I delight greatly in the LORD; my soul rejoices in my God. For he has clothed me with garments of salvation and arrayed me in a robe of righteousness, as a bridegroom adorns his head like a priest, and as a bride adorns herself with her jewels.

Isaiah 61:10

Jesus said, "I will see you again and you will rejoice, and no one will take away your joy."

John 16:22

Go, eat your food with gladness, and drink your wine with a joyful heart, for it is now that God favors what you do.

Ecclesiastes 9:7

In the presence of the LORD your God, you and your families shall eat and shall rejoice in everything you have put your hand to, because the LORD your God has blessed you.

Deuteronomy 12:7

We rejoice in the hope of the glory of God....
We also rejoice in God through our Lord Jesus
Christ, through whom we have now received
reconciliation.

Romans 5:2, 11

Rejoice and be glad, because great is your reward
in heaven.

Matthew 5:12

Rejoice that your names are written in heaven.

Luke 10:20

Let the heavens rejoice, let the earth be glad;
>
> let the sea resound, and all that is in it;
>
> let the fields be jubilant, and everything in
>
> them.

Then all the trees of the forest will sing for joy;
>
> they will sing before the LORD, for he comes,
>
> he comes to judge the earth.

He will judge the world in righteousness
>
> and the peoples in his truth.

Psalm 96:11 – 13

May the God of hope fill you with all joy and
peace as you trust in him.

Romans 15:13

Marriage

God created man in his own image, in the image
of God he created him; male and female he created them. God blessed them and said to them,
"Be fruitful and increase in number."

Genesis 1:27–28

Let love and faithfulness never leave you;
    bind them around your neck,
    write them on the tablet of your heart.
Then you will win favor and a good name
    in the sight of God and man.

Proverbs 3:3–4

He who finds a wife finds what is good
    and receives favor from the LORD.

Proverbs 18:22

Wives, . . . be submissive to your husbands so that, if any of them do not believe the word, they may be won over without words by the behavior of their wives, when they see the purity and reverence of your lives.

1 Peter 3:1–2

May the Lord make your love increase and over-flow for each other.

1 Thessalonians 3:12

Jesus said, "Love one another. As I have loved you, so you must love one another. By this all men will know that you are my disciples, if you love one another."

John 13:34–35

The LORD God said, "It is not good for the man to be alone. I will make a helper suitable for him."

Genesis 2:18

Peacemakers who sow in peace raise a harvest of righteousness.

James 3:18

A wife of noble character is her husband's crown.

Proverbs 12:4

This is my prayer: that your love may abound more and more in knowledge and depth of insight, so that you may be able to discern what is best and may be pure and blameless until the day of Christ, filled with the fruit of righteousness that comes through Jesus Christ—to the glory and praise of God.

Philippians 1:9–11

I will betroth you to me forever; I will betroth
you in righteousness and justice, in love and
compassion.

I will betroth you in faithfulness, and you will
acknowledge the Lord.

Hosea 2:19–20

How delightful is your love, my sister, my bride!
How much more pleasing is your love than wine,
and the fragrance of your perfume than any spice!

Song of Songs 4:10

Her children arise and call her blessed;
    her husband also, and he praises her:
"Many women do noble things,
    but you surpass them all."

Proverbs 31:28–29

There is no fear in love. But perfect love drives out fear.

1 John 4:18

No one has ever seen God; but if we love one another, God lives in us and his love is made complete in us.

1 John 4:12

Motherhood

The Lord tends his flock like a shepherd:
    He gathers the lambs in his arms
and carries them close to his heart;
    he gently leads those that have young.

Isaiah 40:11

"Fix these words of mine in your hearts and
minds; tie them as symbols on your hands and
bind them on your foreheads. Teach them to your
children, talking about them when you sit at home
and when you walk along the road, when you lie
down and when you get up. Write them on the
doorframes of your houses and on your gates, so
that your days and the days of your children may
be many in the land," says the Lord.

Deuteronomy 11:18–21

The Lord settles the barren woman in her home
    as a happy mother of children.

Psalm 113:9

Train a child in the way he should go,
    and when he is old he will not turn from it.

Proverbs 22:6

Discipline your son,
    and he will give you peace;
he will bring delight to your soul.

Proverbs 29:17

Children [are a] reward from God.

Psalm 127:3

Repent and be baptized, every one of you, in the
name of Jesus Christ for the forgiveness of your
sins. And you will receive the gift of the Holy
Spirit. The promise is for you and your children
and for all who are far off—for all whom the Lord
our God will call.

Acts 2:38–39

May your father and mother be glad;
    may she who gave you birth rejoice!

Proverbs 23:25

May the LORD make you increase,
    both you and your children.
May you be blessed by the LORD,
    the Maker of heaven and earth.

Psalm 115:14–15

"As a mother comforts her child,
so will I comfort you," says the Lord.

Isaiah 66:13

Children's children are a crown to the aged,
and parents are the pride of their children.

Proverbs 17:6

You shall rejoice in all the good things the LORD
your God has given to you and your household.

Deuteronomy 26:11

Honor your father and your mother, as the LORD
your God has commanded you, so that you may
live long and that it may go well with you in the
land the LORD your God is giving you.

Deuteronomy 5:16

Obedience

Keep God's decrees and commands, which I am giving you today, so that it may go well with you and your children after you and that you may live long in the land the LORD your God gives you for all time.

Deuteronomy 4:40

Jesus replied, "If anyone loves me, he will obey my teaching. My Father will love him, and we will come to him and make our home with him."

John 14:23

If you are willing and obedient,
    you will eat the best from the land.

Isaiah 1:19

Whatever you have learned or received or heard from me, or seen in me—put it into practice. And the God of peace will be with you.

Philippians 4:9

When Jesus had finished washing [the disciples'] feet, he put on his clothes and returned to his place. "Do you understand what I have done for you?" he asked them.

"You call me 'Teacher' and 'Lord,' and rightly so, for that is what I am. Now that I, your Lord and Teacher, have washed your feet, you also should wash one another's feet. I have set you an example that you should do as I have done for you. I tell you the truth, no servant is greater than his master, nor is a messenger greater than the one who sent him. Now that you know these things, you will be blessed if you do them."

John 13:12–17

Jesus said, "If you obey my commands, you will remain in my love, just as I have obeyed my Father's commands and remain in his love."

John 15:10

Jesus said, "Whoever does the will of my Father in heaven is my brother and sister and mother."

Matthew 12:50

Dear friends, if our hearts do not condemn us, we have confidence before God. And we receive from him anything we ask, because we obey his commands and do what pleases him. And this is his command: to believe in the name of his Son, Jesus Christ, and to love one another as he commanded us. Those who obey his commands live in him, and he in them.

1 John 3:21–24

The man who looks intently into the perfect law
that gives freedom, and continues to do this, not
forgetting what he has heard, but doing it — he
will be blessed in what he does.

James 1:25

"If you obey me fully and keep my covenant, then
out of all nations you will be my treasured possession," says the Lord.

Exodus 19:5

The world and its desires pass away, but the man
who does the will of God lives forever.

1 John 2:17

Walk in God's ways, and keep his decrees and
commands, his laws and requirements ... so that
you may prosper in all you do and wherever you go.

1 Kings 2:3

"Obey me, and I will be your God and you will be
my people. Walk in all the ways I command you,
that it may go well with you," says the Lord.

Jeremiah 7:23

Blessed are they who keep God's statutes
    and seek him with all their heart.

Psalm 119:2

This is what the LORD says—
> your Redeemer, the Holy One of Israel:
"I am the LORD your God,
> who teaches you what is best for you,
who directs you in the way you should go."

Isaiah 48:17

"If you follow my decrees and are careful to obey my commands, I will send you rain in its season, and the ground will yield its crops and the trees of the field their fruit. Your threshing will continue until grape harvest and the grape harvest will continue until planting, and you will eat all the food you want and live in safety in your land," says the Lord.

Leviticus 26:3–5

He who obeys instructions guards his life.

Proverbs 19:16

Just as through the disobedience of the one man [Adam] the many were made sinners, so also through the obedience of the one man [Christ] the many will be made righteous.

Romans 5:19

Continue to work out your salvation with fear and trembling, for it is God who works in you to will and to act according to his good purpose.

Philippians 2:12–13

Obey your leaders and submit to their authority. They keep watch over you as men who must give an account. Obey them so that their work will be a joy, not a burden, for that would be of no advantage to you.

Hebrews 13:17

Men will praise God for the obedience that accompanies your confession of the gospel of Christ.

2 Corinthians 9:13

If anyone obeys his word, God's love is truly made complete in him.

1 John 2:5

Your statutes are wonderful, Lord;
    therefore I obey them....
I obey your statutes,
    for I love them greatly.

Psalm 119:129, 167

Patience

Be patient ... until the Lord's coming. See how the farmer waits for the land to yield its valuable crop and how patient he is for the autumn and spring rains. You too, be patient and stand firm, because the Lord's coming is near.

James 5:7–8

The Lord is not slow in keeping his promise, as some understand slowness. He is patient with you, not wanting anyone to perish, but everyone to come to repentance.

2 Peter 3:9

The fruit of the Spirit is love, joy, peace, patience, kindness, goodness, faithfulness, gentleness and self-control.

Galatians 5:22–23

I wait for you, O LORD;
    you will answer, O Lord my God.

Psalm 38:15

A man's wisdom gives him patience;
    it is to his glory to overlook an offense.

Proverbs 19:11

Through patience a ruler can be persuaded.

Proverbs 25:15

In the morning, O LORD,
    you hear my voice;
in the morning I lay my requests before you
    and wait in expectation.

Psalm 5:3

We pray ... in order that you may live a life worthy of the Lord and may please him in every way: bearing fruit in every good work, growing in the knowledge of God, being strengthened with all power according to his glorious might so that you may have great endurance and patience, and joyfully giving thanks to the Father, who has qualified you to share in the inheritance of the saints in the kingdom of light.

Colossians 1:10–12

I waited patiently for the LORD;
    he turned to me and heard my cry.

Psalm 40:1

Jesus said, "Since you have kept my command to endure patiently, I will also keep you from the hour of trial that is going to come upon the whole world to test those who live on the earth."

Revelation 3:10

Let us hold unswervingly to the hope we profess, for he who promised is faithful.

Hebrews 10:23

I watch in hope for the LORD, I wait for God my Savior; my God will hear me.

Micah 7:7

Christ was sacrificed once to take away the sins of many people; and he will appear a second time, not to bear sin, but to bring salvation to those who are waiting for him.

Hebrews 9:28

I was shown mercy so that in me, the worst of sinners, Christ Jesus might display his unlimited patience as an example for those who would believe on him and receive eternal life.

1 Timothy 1:16

Bear in mind that our Lord's patience means salvation.

2 Peter 3:15

A patient man has great understanding.

Proverbs 14:29

Peace

The LORD gives strength to his people;
    the LORD blesses his people with peace.

Psalm 29:11

No discipline seems pleasant at the time, but painful. Later on, however, it produces a harvest of righteousness and peace for those who have been trained by it.

Hebrews 12:11

Christ himself is our peace, who has made the two one and has destroyed the barrier, the dividing wall of hostility, by abolishing in his flesh the law with its commandments and regulations. His purpose was to create in himself one new man out of the two, thus making peace, and in this one body to reconcile both of them to God through the cross, by which he put to death their hostility. He came and preached peace to you who were far away and peace to those who were near.

Ephesians 2:14–17

Peacemakers who sow in peace raise a harvest of righteousness.

James 3:18

The mind of sinful man is death, but the mind controlled by the Spirit is life and peace.

Romans 8:6

Since we have been justified through faith, we have peace with God through our Lord Jesus Christ, through whom we have gained access by faith into this grace in which we now stand. And we rejoice in the hope of the glory of God.

Romans 5:1–2

Jesus said, "Peace I leave with you; my peace I give you. I do not give to you as the world gives. Do not let your hearts be troubled and do not be afraid."

John 14:27

Perseverance

Perseverance must finish its work so that you may be mature and complete, not lacking anything.

James 1:4

As you know, we consider blessed those who have persevered. You have heard of Job's perseverance and have seen what the Lord finally brought about. The Lord is full of compassion and mercy.

James 5:11

You need to persevere so that when you have done the will of God, you will receive what he has promised.

Hebrews 10:36

Blessed is the man who perseveres under trial, because when he has stood the test, he will receive the crown of life that God has promised to those who love him.

James 1:12

It is God who makes ... you stand firm in Christ.

2 Corinthians 1:21–22

Dear children, continue in Christ, so that when he appears we may be confident and unashamed before him at his coming.

1 John 2:28

Jesus said, "He who stands firm to the end will be saved."

Mark 13:13

Do not be afraid. Stand firm and you will see the deliverance the LORD will bring you today.

Exodus 14:13

Let us acknowledge the LORD;
    let us press on to acknowledge him.
As surely as the sun rises, he will appear;
    he will come to us like the winter rains,
like the spring rains that water the earth.

Hosea 6:3

Not that I have already ... been made perfect, but
I press on to take hold of that for which Christ
Jesus took hold of me. Brothers, I do not consider
myself yet to have taken hold of it. But one thing
I do: Forgetting what is behind and straining
toward what is ahead, I press on toward the goal to
win the prize for which God has called me heaven-
ward in Christ Jesus.

Philippians 3:12–14

We rejoice in the hope of the glory of God. Not only so, but we also rejoice in our sufferings, because we know that suffering produces perseverance; perseverance, character; and character, hope.

Romans 5:2–4

Since we are surrounded by such a great cloud of witnesses, let us throw off everything that hinders and the sin that so easily entangles, and let us run with perseverance the race marked out for us. Let us fix our eyes on Jesus, the author and perfecter of our faith, who for the joy set before him endured the cross, scorning its shame, and sat down at the right hand of the throne of God. Consider him who endured such opposition from sinful men, so that you will not grow weary and lose heart.

Hebrews 12:1–3

Let us not become weary in doing good, for at the proper time we will reap a harvest if we do not give up.

Galatians 6:9

Stand firm. Let nothing move you. Always give yourselves fully to the work of the Lord, because you know that your labor in the Lord is not in vain.

1 Corinthians 15:58

You will keep in perfect peace him whose mind is steadfast, because he trusts in you, Lord.

Isaiah 26:3

The God of all grace, who called you to his eternal glory in Christ, after you have suffered a little while, will himself restore you and make you strong, firm and steadfast. To him be the power for ever and ever. Amen.

1 Peter 5:10–11

Praise and Worship

Come, let us bow down in worship,
   let us kneel before the LORD our Maker.
For he is our God
   and we are the people of his pasture,
the flock under his care.

Psalm 95:6–7

Since we are receiving a kingdom that cannot be
shaken, let us be thankful, and so worship God
acceptably with reverence and awe.

Hebrews 12:28

From the lips of children and infants
   you have ordained praise, O Lord.

Psalm 8:2

Praise be to the God and Father of our Lord Jesus
Christ, who has blessed us in the heavenly realms
with every spiritual blessing in Christ.

Ephesians 1:3

Enter his gates with thanksgiving
    and his courts with praise;
    give thanks to him and praise his name.
For the LORD is good and his love endures forever;
    his faithfulness continues through all
generations.

Psalm 100:4–5

I will praise you with the harp
    for your faithfulness, O my God;
I will sing praise to you with the lyre,
    O Holy One of Israel.
My lips will shout for joy
    when I sing praise to you—
    I, whom you have redeemed.

Psalm 71:22–23

Whenever the living creatures give glory, honor
and thanks to God who sits on the throne and
who lives for ever and ever, the twenty-four elders
fall down before him who sits on the throne, and
worship him who lives for ever and ever. They lay
their crowns before the throne and say:
"You are worthy, our Lord and God,
    to receive glory and honor and power,
for you created all things,
    and by your will they were created
    and have their being."

Revelation 4:9–11

Let them praise his name with dancing
    and make music to him with tambourine and
        harp.
For the LORD takes delight in his people;
    he crowns the humble with salvation.
Let the saints rejoice in this honor
    and sing for joy on their beds.

Psalm 149:3–5

Prayer

Jesus said, "If you remain in me and my words remain in you, ask whatever you wish, and it will be given you."

John 15:7

Whatever you ask for in prayer, believe that you have received it, and it will be yours.

Mark 11:24

The prayer of a righteous man is powerful and effective.

James 5:16

The righteous cry out,
    and the LORD hears them;
he delivers them from all their troubles.

Psalm 34:17

I call to God,
> and the LORD saves me.
Evening, morning and noon I cry out in distress,
> and he hears my voice.

Psalm 55:16–17

Jesus said, "Ask and it will be given to you; seek
and you will find; knock and the door will be
opened to you. For everyone who asks receives; he
who seeks finds; and to him who knocks, the door
will be opened."

Matthew 7:7–8

"Before [my people] call I will answer; while they
are still speaking I will hear," says the Lord.

Isaiah 65:24

"Call to me and I will answer you and tell you great and unsearchable things you do not know," says the Lord.

Jeremiah 33:3

The Spirit helps us in our weakness. We do not know what we ought to pray for, but the Spirit himself intercedes for us with groans that words cannot express.

Romans 8:26

Is any one of you in trouble? He should pray. Is anyone happy? Let him sing songs of praise. Is any one of you sick? He should call the elders of the church to pray over him and anoint him with oil in the name of the Lord. And the prayer offered in faith will make the sick person well; the Lord will raise him up.

James 5:13 – 15

Jesus said, "If two of you on earth agree about anything you ask for, it will be done for you by my Father in heaven."

Matthew 18:19

Jesus said, "If you believe, you will receive whatever you ask for in prayer."

Matthew 21:22

This is the confidence we have in approaching God: that if we ask anything according to his will, he hears us. And if we know that he hears us— whatever we ask—we know that we have what we asked of him.

1 John 5:14–15

Jesus said, "I tell you the truth, my Father will give you whatever you ask in my name. Until now you have not asked for anything in my name. Ask and you will receive, and your joy will be complete."

John 16:23–24

The LORD is near to all who call on him,
    to all who call on him in truth.

Psalm 145:18

"They will call on my name and I will answer them; I will say, 'They are my people,' and they will say, 'The LORD is our God,'" says the Lord.

Zechariah 13:9

In the morning, O LORD, you hear my voice;
    in the morning I lay my requests before you
    and wait in expectation.

Psalm 5:3

How gracious God will be when you cry for help!
As soon as he hears, he will answer you.

Isaiah 30:19

We have confidence before God and receive from
him anything we ask, because we obey his commands and do what pleases him.

1 John 3:21 – 22

"You will call upon me and come and pray to me, and I will listen to you. You will seek me and find me when you seek me with all your heart," says the Lord.

Jeremiah 29:12–13

Jesus said, "I will do whatever you ask in my name, so that the Son may bring glory to the Father. You may ask me for anything in my name, and I will do it."

John 14:13–14

Presence of God

You hem me in — behind and before;
    you have laid your hand upon me.
Such knowledge is too wonderful for me,
    too lofty for me to attain.
Where can I go from your Spirit?
    Where can I flee from your presence?
If I go up to the heavens, you are there;
    if I make my bed in the depths, you are there.
If I rise on the wings of the dawn,
    if I settle on the far side of the sea,
even there your hand will guide me,
    your right hand will hold me fast.

Psalm 139:5 – 10

"My Presence will go with you, and I will give you rest," says the Lord.

Exodus 33:14

In the presence of the LORD your God, you and
your families shall eat and shall rejoice in everything you have put your hand to, because the
LORD your God has blessed you.

Deuteronomy 12:7

You have made known to me
    the path of life, Lord;
you will fill me with joy in your presence,
with eternal pleasures at your right hand.

Psalm 16:11

In my integrity you uphold me
    and set me in your presence forever, Lord.

Psalm 41:12

Blessed are those who have learned to acclaim you,
    who walk in the light of your presence, O
LORD.

Psalm 89:15

You will call, and the LORD will answer;
  you will cry for help, and he will say: Here
    am I.

Isaiah 58:9

In God we live and move and have our being.

Acts 17:28

The LORD is with you when you are with him. If
you seek him, he will be found by you.

2 Chronicles 15:2

Jesus said, "Surely I am with you always, to the
very end of the age."

Matthew 28:20

Jesus said, "Here I am! I stand at the door and knock. If anyone hears my voice and opens the door, I will come in and eat with him, and he with me."

Revelation 3:20

Jesus said, "Where two or three come together in my name, there am I with them."

Matthew 18:20

Surely goodness and love will follow me
    all the days of my life,
and I will dwell in the house of the LORD forever.

Psalm 23:6

Jesus said, "I am the vine; you are the branches.
If a man remains in me and I in him, he will bear much fruit."

John 15:5

One thing I ask of the LORD,
    this is what I seek:
that I may dwell in the house of the LORD
    all the days of my life,
to gaze upon the beauty of the LORD
    and to seek him in his temple.

Psalm 27:4

Blessed are those who dwell in your house, Lord;
    they are ever praising you.

Psalm 84:4

Even though I walk
    through the valley of the shadow of death,
I will fear no evil,
    for you are with me, Lord;
your rod and your staff,
    they comfort me.

Psalm 23:4

You have delivered me from death, Lord,
    and my feet from stumbling,
that I may walk before God
    in the light of life.

Psalm 56:13

I pray that out of God's glorious riches he may strengthen you with power through his Spirit in your inner being, so that Christ may dwell in your hearts through faith.

Ephesians 3:16–17

Priorities

Jesus said, "Everyone who hears these words of mine and puts them into practice is like a wise man who built his house on the rock. The rain came down, the streams rose, and the winds blew and beat against that house; yet it did not fall, because it had its foundation on the rock."

Matthew 7:24–25

The world and its desires pass away, but the man who does the will of God lives forever.

1 John 2:17

Observe what the LORD your God requires: Walk in his ways, and keep his decrees and commands, his laws and requirements ... so that you may prosper in all you do and wherever you go.

1 Kings 2:3

Blessed are they who maintain justice,
who constantly do what is right.

Psalm 106:3

Store up for yourselves treasures in heaven, where
moth and rust do not destroy, and where thieves
do not break in and steal. For where your treasure
is, there your heart will be also.

Matthew 6:20–21

Do not worry, saying, 'What shall we eat?' or
'What shall we drink?' or 'What shall we wear?'
... But seek first God's kingdom and his righteousness, and all these things will be given to you as
well.

Matthew 6:31, 33

As Jesus and his disciples were on their way, he came to a village where a woman named Martha opened her home to him. She had a sister called Mary, who sat at the Lord's feet listening to what he said.

But Martha was distracted by all the preparations that had to be made. She came to him and asked, "Lord, don't you care that my sister has left me to do the work by myself? Tell her to help me!"

"Martha, Martha," the Lord answered, "you are worried and upset about many things, but only one thing is needed. Mary has chosen what is better, and it will not be taken away from her."

Luke 10:38–42

Choose life, so that you and your children may live and that you may love the LORD your God, listen to his voice, and hold fast to him. For the LORD is your life, and he will give you many years in the land he swore to give to your fathers, Abraham, Isaac and Jacob.

Deuteronomy 30:19–20

The LORD your God will make you most prosperous in all the work of your hands and in the fruit of your womb, the young of your livestock and the crops of your land. The LORD will again delight in you and make you prosperous, just as he delighted in your fathers, if you obey the LORD your God and keep his commands and decrees that are written in this Book of the Law and turn to the LORD your God with all your heart and with all your soul.

Deuteronomy 30:9–10

I urge ... that requests, prayers, intercession and thanksgiving be made for everyone—for kings and all those in authority, that we may live peaceful and quiet lives in all godliness and holiness.

1 Timothy 2:1–2

Whatever you do, work at it with all your heart, as working for the Lord, not for men, since you know that you will receive an inheritance from the Lord as a reward. It is the Lord Christ you are serving.

Colossians 3:23–24

Protection

Let all who take refuge in you be glad, O Lord;
    let them ever sing for joy.
Spread your protection over them,
    that those who love your name may rejoice
        in you.
For surely, O LORD, you bless the righteous;
    you surround them with your favor as with a
        shield.

Psalm 5:11–12

You are my hiding place, Lord;
    you will protect me from trouble
and surround me with songs of deliverance.

Psalm 32:7

"Because he loves me," says the LORD, "I will
rescue him;
> I will protect him, for he acknowledges my
> name."

Psalm 91:14

Do not forsake wisdom,
> and she will protect you;
love her,
> and she will watch over you.

Proverbs 4:6

The Lord is faithful, and he will strengthen and
protect you from the evil one.

2 Thessalonians 3:3

The Lord will cover you with his feathers,
> and under his wings you will find refuge;
his faithfulness will be your shield and rampart.

Psalm 91:4

I will lie down and sleep in peace,
    for you alone, O LORD,
make me dwell in safety.

Psalm 4:8

The Lord will command his angels concerning you
    to guard you in all your ways.

Psalm 91:11

Though I walk in the midst of trouble,
    you preserve my life, O Lord.

Psalm 138:7

He is our God
    and we are the people of his pasture,
    the flock under his care.

Psalm 95:7

Your righteousness is like the mighty mountains,
    your justice like the great deep.
O LORD, you preserve both man and beast.
    How priceless is your unfailing love!
Both high and low among men
    find refuge in the shadow of your wings.

Psalm 36:6–7

Whoever listens to [wisdom] will live in safety
    and be at ease, without fear of harm.

Proverbs 1:33

The LORD is a refuge for the oppressed,
    a stronghold in times of trouble.

Psalm 9:9

Taste and see that the LORD is good;
>blessed is the man who takes refuge in him.

Psalm 34:8

I will sing of your strength, O Lord,
>in the morning I will sing of your love;
for you are my fortress,
>my refuge in times of trouble.

Psalm 59:16

May you be richly rewarded by the LORD, the God
of Israel, under whose wings you have come to
take refuge.

Ruth 2:12

Jesus prayed, "I have revealed you to those whom you gave me out of the world. They were yours; you gave them to me and they have obeyed your word. . . . I will remain in the world no longer, but they are still in the world, and I am coming to you. Holy Father, protect them by the power of your name—the name you gave me—so that they may be one as we are one."

John 17:6, 11

When you pass through the waters, I will be with you; and when you pass through the rivers, they will not sweep over you.

When you walk through the fire, you will not be burned; the flames will not set you ablaze.

For I am the Lord, your God.

Isaiah 43:2–3

Provision

God will meet all your needs according to his
glorious riches in Christ Jesus.

Philippians 4:19

You care for the land and water it, Lord;
    you enrich it abundantly.
The streams of God are filled with water
    to provide the people with grain,
for so you have ordained it.

Psalm 65:9

Your kingdom is an everlasting kingdom, O God,
    and your dominion endures through all
        generations.
The LORD is faithful to all his promises
    and loving toward all he has made.

Psalm 145:13

God said [to Abraham], "Take your son, your only son, Isaac, whom you love, and go to the region of Moriah. Sacrifice him there as a burnt offering on one of the mountains I will tell you about."…

When they reached the place God had told him about, Abraham built an altar there and … bound his son Isaac and laid him on the altar … Then he reached out his hand and took the knife to slay his son. But the angel of the LORD called out to him from heaven, "Abraham! Abraham!… Do not lay a hand on the boy," he said. "Do not do anything to him. Now I know that you fear God, because you have not withheld from me your son, your only son."

Abraham looked up and there in a thicket he saw a ram caught by its horns. He went over and took the ram and sacrificed it as a burnt offering instead of his son.

Abraham called that place The LORD Will Provide.

Genesis 22:2, 9–14

All these blessings will come upon you and accompany you if you obey the LORD your God:

You will be blessed in the city and blessed in the country.

The fruit of your womb will be blessed, and the crops of your land and the young of your livestock—the calves of your herds and the lambs of your flocks.

Your basket and your kneading trough will be blessed.

You will be blessed when you come in and blessed when you go out.

The LORD will grant that the enemies who rise up against you will be defeated before you. They will come at you from one direction but flee from you in seven.

The LORD will send a blessing on your barns and on everything you put your hand to. The LORD your God will bless you in the land he is giving you.

Deuteronomy 28:2–8

The LORD covers the sky with clouds;
    he supplies the earth with rain
and makes grass grow on the hills.
He provides food for the cattle
    and for the young ravens when they call.
His pleasure is not in the strength of the horse,
    nor his delight in the legs of a man;
the LORD delights in those who fear him,
    who put their hope in his unfailing love.

Psalm 147:8–11

God who supplies seed to the sower and bread for
food will also supply and increase your store of
seed and will enlarge the harvest of your righteousness. You will be made rich in every way so that
you can be generous on every occasion, and . . .
your generosity will result in thanksgiving to God.

2 Corinthians 9:10–11

You still the hunger of those you cherish, Lord;
    their sons have plenty,
and they store up wealth for their children.

Psalm 17:14

Jesus said, "Do not worry about your life, what
you will eat or drink; or about your body, what
you will wear. Is not life more important than
food, and the body more important than clothes?
Look at the birds of the air; they do not sow or
reap or store away in barns, and yet your heavenly
Father feeds them. Are you not much more valuable than they?... But seek first his kingdom and
his righteousness, and all these things will be given
to you as well."

Matthew 6:25–26, 33

Blessed are all who fear the LORD,
  who walk in his ways.
You will eat the fruit of your labor;
  blessings and prosperity will be yours....
Your sons will be like olive shoots around
    your table.
  Thus is the man blessed who fears the LORD.

Psalm 128:1 – 4

God is able to make all grace abound to you, so
that in all things at all times, having all that you
need, you will abound in every good work.

2 Corinthians 9:8

Praise be to the God and Father of our Lord Jesus
Christ, the Father of compassion and the God of
all comfort, who comforts us in all our troubles, so
that we can comfort those in any trouble with the
comfort we ourselves have received from God.

2 Corinthians 1:3–4

The Lord will love you and bless you and increase
your numbers. He will bless the fruit of your
womb, the crops of your land—your grain, new
wine and oil—the calves of your herds and the
lambs of your flocks in the land that he swore to
your forefathers to give you.

Deuteronomy 7:13

The LORD is my shepherd, I shall not be in want.

Psalm 23:1

The lions may grow weak and hungry,
>   but those who seek the LORD lack no good
>   thing.

Psalm 34:10

Fear the LORD, you his saints,
>   for those who fear him lack nothing.

Psalm 34:9

Give, and it will be given to you. A good measure,
pressed down, shaken together and running over,
will be poured into your lap. For with the measure
you use, it will be measured to you.

Luke 6:38

"Bring the whole tithe into the storehouse, that
there may be food in my house. Test me in this,"
says the LORD Almighty, "and see if I will not
throw open the floodgates of heaven and pour
out so much blessing that you will not have room
enough for it."

Malachi 3:10

I was young and now I am old,
> yet I have never seen the righteous forsaken
> or their children begging bread.
They are always generous and lend freely;
> their children will be blessed.

Psalm 37:25–26

Remember this: Whoever sows sparingly will also reap sparingly, and whoever sows generously will also reap generously. Each man should give what he has decided in his heart to give, not reluctantly or under compulsion, for God loves a cheerful giver.

2 Corinthians 9:6–7

Now to God who is able to do immeasurably more than all we ask or imagine, according to his power that is at work within us to him be glory in the church and in Christ Jesus throughout all generations, for ever and ever! Amen.

Ephesians 3:20–21

Rest

Jesus said, "Come to me, all you who are weary
and burdened, and I will give you rest. Take my
yoke upon you and learn from me, for I am gentle
and humble in heart, and you will find rest for
your souls."

Matthew 11:28–29

"My people will live in peaceful dwelling places,
    in secure homes,
in undisturbed places of rest," says the Lord.

Isaiah 32:18

The LORD says, "My Presence will go with you,
and I will give you rest."

Exodus 33:14

My soul finds rest in God alone;
> my salvation comes from him.
He alone is my rock and my salvation;
> he is my fortress, I will never be shaken.

Psalm 62:1–2

He who dwells in the shelter of the Most High
> will rest in the shadow of the Almighty.
I will say of the LORD, "He is my refuge and my fortress,
> my God, in whom I trust."

Psalm 91:1–2

The LORD will fight for you; you need only to be still.

Exodus 14:14

The LORD is my shepherd, I shall not be in want.
    He makes me lie down in green pastures,
he leads me beside quiet waters,
    he restores my soul.
He guides me in paths of righteousness
    for his name's sake.

Psalm 23:1–3

The LORD stilled the storm to a whisper;
    the waves of the sea were hushed.
They were glad when it grew calm,
    and he guided them to their desired haven.
Let them give thanks to the LORD for his
        unfailing love
    and his wonderful deeds for men.

Psalm 107:29–31

Stand at the crossroads and look; ask for the ancient paths, ask where the good way is, and walk in it, and you will find rest for your souls.

Jeremiah 6:16

Let the beloved of the LORD rest secure in him, for he shields him all day long, and the one the LORD loves rests between his shoulders.

Deuteronomy 33:12

The fear of the LORD leads to life:
    Then one rests content, untouched by trouble.

Proverbs 19:23

The LORD is the everlasting God,
the Creator of the ends of the earth.
He will not grow tired or weary,
and his understanding no one can fathom.
He gives strength to the weary
and increases the power of the weak.
Even youths grow tired and weary,
and young men stumble and fall;
but those who hope in the LORD
will renew their strength.
They will soar on wings like eagles;
they will run and not grow weary,
they will walk and not be faint.

Isaiah 40:28–31

I will lie down and sleep in peace,
    for you alone, O LORD,
make me dwell in safety.

Psalm 4:8

The LORD your God is with you,
    he is mighty to save.
He will take great delight in you,
    he will quiet you with his love,
he will rejoice over you with singing.

Zephaniah 3:17

There remains, . . . a Sabbath-rest for the people of
God; for anyone who enters God's rest also rests
from his own work, just as God did from his. Let
us, therefore, make every effort to enter that rest.

Hebrews 4:9–11

This is what the Sovereign LORD, the Holy One of
    Israel, says:
"In repentance and rest is your salvation,
    in quietness and trust is your strength."

Isaiah 30:15

Do not be anxious about anything, but in everything, by prayer and petition, with thanksgiving,
present your requests to God. And the peace of
God, which transcends all understanding, will
guard your hearts and your minds in Christ Jesus.

Philippians 4:6–7

My heart is glad and my tongue rejoices;
    my body also will rest secure,
because you will not abandon me to the grave,
      O LORD,
    nor will you let your Holy One see decay.

Psalm 16:9–10

God grants sleep to those he loves.

Psalm 127:2

I lie down and sleep;
> I wake again, because the LORD sustains me.

Psalm 3:5

The God of all grace, who called you to his eternal glory in Christ, after you have suffered a little while, will himself restore you and make you strong, firm and steadfast.

1 Peter 5:10

Salvation

God so loved the world that he gave his one and only Son, that whoever believes in him shall not perish but have eternal life. For God did not send his Son into the world to condemn the world, but to save the world through him. Whoever believes in him is not condemned.

John 3:16–18

We have seen and testify that the Father has sent his Son to be the Savior of the world. If anyone acknowledges that Jesus is the Son of God, God lives in him and he in God.

1 John 4:14–15

Christ was sacrificed once to take away the sins of many people; and he will appear a second time, not to bear sin, but to bring salvation to those who are waiting for him.

Hebrews 9:28

I trust in your unfailing love, O God;
    my heart rejoices in your salvation.
I will sing to the LORD,
    for he has been good to me.

Psalm 13:5–6

The LORD is my light and my salvation—
    whom shall I fear?
The LORD is the stronghold of my life—
    of whom shall I be afraid?

Psalm 27:1

Because Jesus lives forever, he has a permanent
priesthood. Therefore he is able to save completely
those who come to God through him, because he
always lives to intercede for them.

Hebrews 7:24–25

The salvation of the righteous comes from the
>   LORD;
>   he is their stronghold in time of trouble.

Psalm 37:39

Jesus said to him, "The Son of Man came to seek
and to save what was lost."

Luke 19:10

The Lord will rescue me from every evil attack
and will bring me safely to his heavenly kingdom.
To him be glory for ever and ever.

2 Timothy 4:18

God did not appoint us to suffer wrath but to
receive salvation through our Lord Jesus Christ.
He died for us so that, whether we are awake or
asleep, we may live together with him.

1 Thessalonians 5:9–10

You ... were included in Christ when you heard
the word of truth, the gospel of your salvation.
Having believed, you were marked in him with
a seal, the promised Holy Spirit, who is a deposit
guaranteeing our inheritance until the redemption
of those who are God's possession — to the praise
of his glory.

Ephesians 1:13–14

Surely God is my salvation; I will trust and not be afraid. The LORD, the LORD, is my strength and my song; he has become my salvation. With joy you will draw water from the wells of salvation.

Isaiah 12:2–3

Everyone who calls on the name of the Lord will be saved.

Romans 10:13

Jesus said, "I am the gate; whoever enters through me will be saved. He will come in and go out, and find pasture."

John 10:9

The LORD will be the sure foundation for your times, a rich store of salvation and wisdom and knowledge; the fear of the LORD is the key to this treasure.

Isaiah 33:6

I am not ashamed of the gospel, because it is the power of God for the salvation of everyone who believes.

Romans 1:16

If you confess with your mouth, "Jesus is Lord," and believe in your heart that God raised him from the dead, you will be saved.

Romans 10:9

Our God is a God who saves.

Psalm 68:20

Jesus said, "My Father's will is that everyone who looks to the Son and believes in him shall have eternal life, and I will raise him up at the last day."

John 6:40

Whoever believes in the Son has eternal life.

John 3:36

Jesus said, "Whoever drinks the water I give him will never thirst. Indeed, the water I give him will become in him a spring of water welling up to eternal life."

John 4:14

Sing to the LORD a new song,
>   for he has done marvelous things;
his right hand and his holy arm
>   have worked salvation for him.
The LORD has made his salvation known
>   and revealed his righteousness to the nations.
He has remembered his love
>   and his faithfulness to the house of Israel;
all the ends of the earth have seen
>   the salvation of our God.

Psalm 98:1–3

Jesus said "I tell you the truth, whoever hears my word and believes him who sent me has eternal life and will not be condemned; he has crossed over from death to life."

John 5:24

Though you have not seen Christ, you love him;
and even though you do not see him now, you
believe in him and are filled with an inexpressible
and glorious joy, for you are receiving the goal of
your faith, the salvation of your souls.

1 Peter 1:8–9

Jesus said, "My sheep listen to my voice; I know
them, and they follow me. I give them eternal life,
and they shall never perish; no one can snatch
them out of my hand. My Father, who has given
them to me, is greater than all; no one can snatch
them out of my Father's hand."

John 10:27–29

Security

Let the beloved of the LORD rest secure in him,
for he shields him all day long.

Deuteronomy 33:12

In the day of trouble
the Lord will keep me safe in his dwelling;
he will hide me in the shelter of his tabernacle
and set me high upon a rock.

Psalm 27:5

Trust in the LORD and do good;
dwell in the land and enjoy safe pasture.
Delight yourself in the LORD
and he will give you the desires of your heart.

Psalm 37:3–4

The name of the LORD is a strong tower;
   the righteous run to it and are safe.

Proverbs 18:10

Preserve sound judgment and discernment,
   do not let them out of your sight;
they will be life for you,
   an ornament to grace your neck.
Then you will go on your way in safety,
   and your foot will not stumble.

Proverbs 3:21–23

Let all who take refuge in you be glad, Lord;
   let them ever sing for joy.
Spread your protection over them,
   that those who love your name may rejoice
      in you.

Psalm 5:11

"Because he loves me," says the LORD, "I will
      rescue him;
  I will protect him, for he acknowledges my
      name."

Psalm 91:14

Discretion will protect you,
  and understanding will guard you.

Proverbs 2:11

Jesus prayed [for his followers], "My prayer is not
that you take them out of the world but that you
protect them from the evil one."

John 17:15

LORD, you have assigned me my portion and
      my cup;
  you have made my lot secure.

Psalm 16:5

My God is my rock, in whom I take refuge, my
shield and the horn of my salvation. He is my
stronghold, my refuge and my savior.

2 Samuel 22:3

The Lord holds victory in store for the upright,
    he is a shield to those whose walk is blameless,
for he guards the course of the just
    and protects the way of his faithful ones.

Proverbs 2:7–8

The eternal God is your refuge,
    and underneath are the everlasting arms.

Deuteronomy 33:27

He who fears the LORD has a secure fortress,
    and for his children it will be a refuge.

Proverbs 14:26

Good will come to him who is generous and lends
     freely,
   who conducts his affairs with justice.
Surely he will never be shaken;
   a righteous man will be remembered forever.
He will have no fear of bad news;
   his heart is steadfast, trusting in the LORD.
His heart is secure, he will have no fear;
   in the end he will look in triumph on his foes.

Psalm 112:5–8

Because God wanted to make the unchanging
nature of his purpose very clear to the heirs of
what was promised, he confirmed it with an oath.
God did this so that, by two unchangeable things
in which it is impossible for God to lie, we who
have fled to take hold of the hope offered to us
may be greatly encouraged. We have this hope as
an anchor for the soul, firm and secure.

Hebrews 6:17–19

I am convinced that neither death nor life, neither angels nor demons, neither the present nor the future, nor any powers, neither height nor depth, nor anything else in all creation, will be able to separate us from the love of God that is in Christ Jesus our Lord.

Romans 8:38–39

Jesus said, "My sheep listen to my voice; I know them, and they follow me. I give them eternal life, and they shall never perish; no one can snatch them out of my hand. My Father, who has given them to me, is greater than all; no one can snatch them out of my Father's hand."

John 10:27–29

God anointed us, set his seal of ownership on us, and put his Spirit in our hearts as a deposit, guaranteeing what is to come.

2 Corinthians 1:21–22

Let us draw near to God with a sincere heart in full assurance of faith, having our hearts sprinkled to cleanse us from a guilty conscience and having our bodies washed with pure water.

Hebrews 10:22

Since we have a great high priest who has gone through the heavens, Jesus the Son of God, let us hold firmly to the faith we profess. For we do not have a high priest who is unable to sympathize with our weaknesses, but we have one who has been tempted in every way, just as we are — yet was without sin.

Hebrews 4:14 – 15

If the LORD delights in a man's way,
    he makes his steps firm;
though he stumble, he will not fall,
    for the LORD upholds him with his hand.

Psalm 37:23 – 24

God's solid foundation stands firm, sealed with this inscription: "The Lord knows those who are his."

2 Timothy 2:19

Jesus said, "Everyone who hears these words of mine and puts them into practice is like a wise man who built his house on the rock. The rain came down, the streams rose, and the winds blew and beat against that house; yet it did not fall, because it had its foundation on the rock.

Matthew 7:24–25

Strength

The LORD is my strength and my song; he has become my salvation. He is my God, and I will praise him, my father's God, and I will exalt him.

Exodus 15:2

In your unfailing love you will lead the people you have redeemed, O Lord. In your strength you will guide them to your holy dwelling.

Exodus 15:13

It is God who arms me with strength and makes my way perfect.

2 Samuel 22:33

The LORD is my strength and my shield;
    my heart trusts in him, and I am helped.
My heart leaps for joy
    and I will give thanks to him in song.
The LORD is the strength of his people,
    a fortress of salvation for his anointed one.

Psalm 28:7–8

The LORD gives strength to his people;
    the LORD blesses his people with peace.

Psalm 29:11

God is our refuge and strength,
    an ever-present help in trouble.

Psalm 46:1

I can do everything through Christ who gives me strength.

Philippians 4:13

The Lord stood at my side and gave me strength, so that through me the message might be fully proclaimed.

2 Timothy 4:17

The Sovereign LORD is my strength;
   he makes my feet like the feet of a deer,
he enables me to go on the heights.

Habakkuk 3:19

Jesus said, "My grace is sufficient for you, for my power is made perfect in weakness."

2 Corinthians 12:9

The Lord gives strength to the weary and increases the power of the weak. Even youths grow tired and weary, and young men stumble and fall; Those who hope in the LORD will renew their strength.

They will soar on wings like eagles; they will run and not grow weary, they will walk and not be faint.

Isaiah 40:29–31

"I have raised you up for this very purpose, that I might show you my power and that my name might be proclaimed in all the earth," says the Lord.

Exodus 9:16

"I will search for the lost and bring back the strays.
I will bind up the injured and strengthen the
weak," says the Lord.

Ezekiel 34:16

May our Lord Jesus Christ himself and God our
Father, who loved us and by his grace gave us
eternal encouragement and good hope, encourage
your hearts and strengthen you in every good deed
and word.

2 Thessalonians 2:16–17

The eyes of the LORD range throughout the earth
to strengthen those whose hearts are fully committed to him.

2 Chronicles 16:9

"I will strengthen them in the LORD and in his name they will walk," declares the LORD.

Zechariah 10:12

I pray that out of his glorious riches God may strengthen you with power through his Spirit in your inner being, so that Christ may dwell in your hearts through faith.

Ephesians 3:16–17

The joy of the LORD is your strength.

Nehemiah 8:10

Trust

Trust in the LORD with all your heart
    and lean not on your own understanding;
in all your ways acknowledge him,
    and he will make your paths straight.

Proverbs 3:5–6

Trust in the LORD and do good;
    dwell in the land and enjoy safe pasture.
Delight yourself in the LORD
    and he will give you the desires of your heart.

Psalm 37:3–4

Those who know your name will trust in you,
    for you, LORD, have never forsaken those who
seek you.

Psalm 9:10

The LORD is good, a refuge in times of trouble. He cares for those who trust in him.

Nahum 1:7

May the God of hope fill you with all joy and peace as you trust in him, so that you may overflow with hope by the power of the Holy Spirit.

Romans 15:13

Blessed is the man who trusts in the LORD, whose confidence is in him. He will be like a tree planted by the water that sends out its roots by the stream. It does not fear when heat comes; its leaves are always green. It has no worries in a year of drought and never fails to bear fruit.

Jeremiah 17:7–8

Surely this is our God; we trusted in him, and he saved us. This is the LORD, we trusted in him; let us rejoice and be glad in his salvation.

Isaiah 25:9

I am like an olive tree flourishing in the house
      of God;
    I trust in God's unfailing love for ever and
      ever.

Psalm 52:8

When I am afraid,
    I will trust in you.
In God, whose word I praise,
    in God I trust; I will not be afraid.
What can mortal man do to me?

Psalm 56:3–4

He who dwells in the shelter of the Most High
will rest in the shadow of the Almighty.
I will say of the LORD, "He is my refuge and my
fortress,
my God, in whom I trust."

Psalm 91:1–2

In Scripture it says:
"See, I lay a stone in Zion,
a chosen and precious cornerstone,
and the one who trusts in him
will never be put to shame."

1 Peter 2:6

Unity

How good and pleasant it is
  when brothers live together in unity!
It is like precious oil poured on the head,
  running down on the beard,
running down on Aaron's beard,
  down upon the collar of his robes.
It is as if the dew of Hermon
  were falling on Mount Zion.
For there the LORD bestows his blessing,
  even life forevermore.

Psalm 133:1–3

A man will leave his father and mother and be
united to his wife, and the two will become one
flesh ... they are no longer two, but one. Therefore what God has joined together, let man not
separate.

Matthew 19:5–6

Jesus prayed, "My prayer is not for [my disciples] alone. I pray also for those who will believe in me through their message, that all of them may be one, Father, just as you are in me and I am in you. May they also be in us so that the world may believe that you have sent me. I have given them the glory that you gave me, that they may be one as we are one: I in them and you in me. May they be brought to complete unity to let the world know that you sent me and have loved them even as you have loved me."

John 17:20–23

Be of one mind, live in peace. And the God of love and peace will be with you.

2 Corinthians 13:11

You are no longer foreigners and aliens, but fellow citizens with God's people and members of God's household, built on the foundation of the apostles and prophets, with Christ Jesus himself as the chief cornerstone. In Christ the whole building is joined together and rises to become a holy temple in the Lord. And in him you too are being built together to become a dwelling in which God lives by his Spirit.

Ephesians 2:19–22

Jesus said, "By this all men will know that you are my disciples, if you love one another."

John 13:35

Jesus said, "Blessed are the peacemakers, for they will be called sons of God."

Matthew 5:9

Jesus said, "Where two or three come together in my name, there am I with them."

Matthew 18:20

The body is a unit, though it is made up of many parts; and though all its parts are many, they form one body. So it is with Christ. For we were all baptized by one Spirit into one body—whether Jews or Greeks, slave or free—and we were all given the one Spirit to drink.

1 Corinthians 12:12–13

Peacemakers who sow in peace raise a harvest of righteousness.

James 3:18

Jesus prayed, "Holy Father, protect [my followers] by the power of your name—the name you gave me—so that they may be one as we are one."

John 17:11

May the God who gives endurance and encouragement give you a spirit of unity among yourselves as you follow Christ Jesus, so that with one heart and mouth you may glorify the God and Father of our Lord Jesus Christ.

Romans 15:5–6

Wisdom

By wisdom a house is built,
    and through understanding it is established;
through knowledge its rooms are filled
    with rare and beautiful treasures.

Proverbs 24:3–4

If any of you lacks wisdom, he should ask God,
who gives generously to all without finding fault,
and it will be given to him.

James 1:5

Surely you desire truth in the inner parts;
    you teach me wisdom in the inmost place,
        O Lord.

Psalm 51:6

The fear of the Lord is the beginning of wisdom;
    all who follow his precepts have good
        understanding.
To him belongs eternal praise.

Psalm 111:10

If you accept my words
    and store up my commands within you,
turning your ear to wisdom
    and applying your heart to understanding,
and if you call out for insight
    and cry aloud for understanding,
and if you look for it as for silver
    and search for it as for hidden treasure,
then you will understand the fear of the Lord
    and find the knowledge of God.

Proverbs 2:1 – 5

Blessed is the man who finds wisdom,
    the man who gains understanding,
for she is more profitable than silver
    and yields better returns than gold.

Proverbs 3:13–14

He who gets wisdom loves his own soul;
    he who cherishes understanding prospers.

Proverbs 19:8

A man's wisdom gives him patience;
    it is to his glory to overlook an offense.

Proverbs 19:11

The fruit of the righteous is a tree of life,
    and he who wins souls is wise.

Proverbs 11:30

Wisdom is supreme; therefore get wisdom.
Though it cost all you have, get understanding.
Esteem her, and she will exalt you;
embrace her, and she will honor you.
She will set a garland of grace on your head
and present you with a crown of splendor.

Proverbs 4:7–9

Wisdom calls,
"Listen to my instruction and be wise;
do not ignore it.
Blessed is the man who listens to me,
watching daily at my doors,
waiting at my doorway.
For whoever finds me finds life
and receives favor from the LORD."

Proverbs 8:33–35

The teaching of the wise is a fountain of life.

Proverbs 13:14

The path of life leads upward for the wise.

Proverbs 15:24

The wise in heart are called discerning,
  and pleasant words promote instruction.

Proverbs 16:21

Listen to advice and accept instruction,
  and in the end you will be wise.

Proverbs 19:20

If your heart is wise,
    then my heart will be glad;
my inmost being will rejoice
    when your lips speak what is right.

Proverbs 23:15–16

My purpose is that they may be encouraged in heart and united in love, so that they may have the full riches of complete understanding, in order that they may know the mystery of God, namely, Christ, in whom are hidden all the treasures of wisdom and knowledge.

Colossians 2:2–3

Worry

Jesus said, "Do not worry about your life, what you will eat or drink; or about your body, what you will wear.... Look at the birds of the air; they do not sow or reap or store away in barns, and yet your heavenly Father feeds them. Are you not much more valuable than they?...

"And why do you worry about clothes? See how the lilies of the field grow. They do not labor or spin. Yet I tell you that not even Solomon in all his splendor was dressed like one of these. If that is how God clothes the grass of the field,... will he not much more clothe you?...

"So do not worry, saying, 'What shall we eat?' or 'What shall we drink?' or 'What shall we wear?' For ... your heavenly Father knows that you need them.

But seek first his kingdom and his righteousness, and all these things will be given to you as well.

Matthew 6:25–26, 28–33

Do not be anxious about anything, but in everything, by prayer and petition, with thanksgiving,
present your requests to God. And the peace of
God, which transcends all understanding, will
guard your hearts and your minds in Christ Jesus.

Philippians 4:6–7

When I said, "My foot is slipping,"
     your love, O LORD, supported me.
When anxiety was great within me,
     your consolation brought joy to my soul.

Psalm 94:18–19

"Though the mountains be shaken
     and the hills be removed,
yet my unfailing love for you will not be shaken
     nor my covenant of peace be removed,"
     says the LORD, who has compassion on you.

Isaiah 54:10

The LORD himself goes before you and will be with you; he will never leave you nor forsake you. Do not be afraid; do not be discouraged.

Deuteronomy 31:8

Let us ... approach the throne of grace with confidence, so that we may receive mercy and find grace to help us in our time of need.

Hebrews 4:16

Jesus said, "Come to me, all you who are weary and burdened, and I will give you rest. Take my yoke upon you and learn from me, for I am gentle and humble in heart, and you will find rest for your souls. For my yoke is easy and my burden is light."

Matthew 11:28–30

Cast your cares on the LORD
    and he will sustain you;
he will never let the righteous fall.

Psalm 55:22

The Lord is my helper; I will not be afraid.
    What can man do to me?

Hebrews 13:6

He who fears the LORD has a secure fortress,
    and for his children it will be a refuge.

Proverbs 14:26

Do not fear, for I am with you;
     do not be dismayed, for I am your God.
I will strengthen you and help you;
     I will uphold you with my righteous right
          hand.

Isaiah 41:10

Cast all your anxiety on God because he cares for you.

1 Peter 5:7

God did not give us a spirit of timidity, but a spirit of power, of love and of self-discipline.

2 Timothy 1:7

Work

The LORD will open the heavens, the storehouse
of his bounty, to send rain on your land in season
and to bless all the work of your hands.

Deuteronomy 28:12

You will ... obey the LORD and follow all his
commands I am giving you today. Then the LORD
your God will make you most prosperous in all
the work of your hands and in the fruit of your
womb, the young of your livestock and the crops
of your land.

Deuteronomy 30:8–9

From the fruit of his lips a man is filled with good
things
    as surely as the work of his hands rewards him.

Proverbs 12:14

All hard work brings a profit.

Proverbs 14:23

Diligent hands will rule.

Proverbs 12:24

Jesus said, "Take my yoke upon you and learn
from me, for I am gentle and humble in heart, and
you will find rest for your souls. For my yoke is
easy and my burden is light."

Matthew 11:29–30

Jesus said to them, "My Father is always at his
work to this very day, and I, too, am working."

John 5:17

The sleep of a laborer is sweet,
    whether he eats little or much.

Ecclesiastes 5:12

Whatever you do, work at it with all your heart, as working for the Lord, not for men, since you know that you will receive an inheritance from the Lord as a reward. It is the Lord Christ you are serving.

Colossians 3:23–24

Stand firm. Let nothing move you. Always give yourselves fully to the work of the Lord, because you know that your labor in the Lord is not in vain.

1 Corinthians 15:58

A wife of noble character who can find?
She is worth far more than rubies.
Her husband has full confidence in her
and lacks nothing of value.
She brings him good, not harm,
    all the days of her life.
She selects wool and flax
    and works with eager hands.
She is like the merchant ships,
    bringing her food from afar.
She gets up while it is still dark;
    she provides food for her family
    and portions for her servant girls.
She considers a field and buys it;
    out of her earnings she plants a vineyard.
She sets about her work vigorously;
    her arms are strong for her tasks.

She sees that her trading is profitable,
    and her lamp does not go out at night.
In her hand she holds the distaff
    and grasps the spindle with her fingers.
She opens her arms to the poor
    and extends her hands to the needy.
When it snows, she has no fear for her household;
    for all of them are clothed in scarlet.
She makes coverings for her bed;
    she is clothed in fine linen and purple.
Her husband is respected at the city gate,
    where he takes his seat among the elders of the
        land.
She makes linen garments and sells them,
    and supplies the merchants with sashes.
She is clothed with strength and dignity;
    she can laugh at the days to come.

She speaks with wisdom,
and faithful instruction is on her tongue.
She watches over the affairs of her household
and does not eat the bread of idleness.
Her children arise and call her blessed;
her husband also, and he praises her:
"Many women do noble things,
but you surpass them all."
Charm is deceptive, and beauty is fleeting;
but a woman who fears the LORD is to be
praised.
Give her the reward she has earned,
and let her works bring her praise at the city
gate.

Proverbs 31:10–31

The one who plants and the one who waters have one purpose, and each will be rewarded according to their own labor. For we are God's fellow workers; you are God's field, God's building.

1 Corinthians 3:8–9

We always thank God for all of you, mentioning you in our prayers. We continually remember before our God and Father your work produced by faith, your labor prompted by love, and your endurance inspired by hope in our Lord Jesus Christ.

1 Thessalonians 1:2–3

The LORD your God will bless you in all your harvest and in all the work of your hands, and your joy will be complete.

Deuteronomy 16:15

Jesus said, "Do not work for food that spoils, but for food that endures to eternal life, which the Son of Man will give you. On him God the Father has placed his seal of approval."

John 6:27

We want to hear from you.
Please send your comments about this
book to us in care of zreview@zondervan.com. Thank you.

ZONDERVAN.com/
AUTHORTRACKER
follow your favorite authors